THE ENERGY
INVESTMENT GAME

The Energy Investment Game: How To Play It And Win With Oil and Gas

By

W. A. Armfield, Jr.

Institute for Business Planning

IBP PLAZA, ENGLEWOOD CLIFFS, N. J. 07632

© Copyright 1981, by Institute for Business Planning, Inc.
IBP Plaza, Englewood Cliffs, NJ 07632

Second Printing. . . . April 1981

Library of Congress Cataloging in Publication Data

Armfield, W   A
   The energy investment game.

   Includes index.
   1. Petroleum industry and trade--United States--Finance.   2.   Gas, Natural--United States--Finance.
I. Title.
HD9565.A75   332.6'722   80-19221
ISBN 0-87624-127-5 (pbk.)

About the Author

W. A. ARMFIELD, Jr., is the President of the Armfield Organization, Inc., a member of the National Association of Securities Dealers. Mr. Armfield has been active in oil and gas financing for more than ten years, including SEC registered programs, private placements, industrial end user programs and as a consultant. For two years he was the instructor in a seminar sponsored by New York University, "Financing Oil and Gas Ventures."

Mr. Armfield attended the University of North Carolina where he was a masters candidate and graduate instructor in the School of Romance Languages. He holds a B.A. in Spanish from Davidson College.

Mr. Armfield was employed by Reynolds & Co., members New York Stock Exchange (now a part of Dean Witter Reynolds, Inc.). He was an Account Executive, Resident Manager of two branch offices and was a member of the corporate finance field staff.

His previous publications include: "How To Sell Oil and Gas Drilling Programs Successfully," Thad Thomas Associates, Inc., published in 1972 and "Investment in Subsidized Housing: Opportunities and Risks," Pilot Books, published in 1979.

Foreword

"EF Hutton & Company has been a leading factor in the oil and gas drilling investment field since 1970 and has raised far in excess of $500,000,000 for drilling activities. We strongly believe that drilling for oil and gas not only presents our high tax bracket investors with the opportunity for significant tax savings but, more importantly, we recognize the possibility for significant increases in assets based on what we believe to be a continued shortage of fossil fuels here in the United States.

Recent events have only served to underscore our original commitment to these risk ventures, and we recommend them to suitable high tax bracket investors wherever possible. I personally believe that oil and gas prices will continue to escalate over the next several years, and high tax bracket investors who carefully select oil and gas companies with whom to drill can still realize significant long term increases in their assets if these ventures are successful. The most recent increases in prices have brought a whole flush of unscrupulous operators into the business who hope to capitalize on the increased interest in oil and gas programs, and we can only recommend that high tax bracket investors double their surveillance while making investments during these trying times in the energy business.

We hope that this book will assist the qualified risk investor in selecting suitable oil and gas investments."

Lawrence J. Winston
Senior Vice President
National Director
Tax Sheltered Investment Programs

A Word From The Author

What you are reading today had its beginning a decade ago. A group of some fifty registered representatives from the N.Y.S.E. member firm of Shearson-Hammill & Company, Inc., was gathered in one of the smaller meeting rooms of the Fairmont Hotel in San Francisco to hear a presentation on the first publicly-registered drilling program to whose prospectus had been affixed the Shearson-Hammill name. The importance of this endorsement, to those of you not in Wall Street, was that the ultimate display of confidence by a major member firm in any kind of underwriting (even a best-efforts offering of this type) was to put the firm's name on the offering circular. What this also meant was, that of the some one-hundred and fifty publicly-offered drilling programs, Shearson had singled out the program I was selling as the vehicle which it deemed most attractive to offer to its clients.

My program had as its general partners a Big Board listed company in the Southeast and a substantial independent oil operator out of Texas. The meeting was just about to start when a resounding crash from the double doors to the right turned everyone's head. Following the crash, the double doors swung open to reveal a highly-polished Datsun just out of the crate. The crew rolling the car to a Datsun dealer's meeting in the adjoining meeting room had not only picked the wrong room, but in their rush to get the car into the meeting, had shoved it into the closed door. So my career as a drilling program salesman really did begin with a crash, which only served to double the number of knots in my stomach. Shearson knew that the General Partners had never run a drilling program before, but they knew also of the AAAA financial status and the excellent reputation of the General Partners. By almost the same token, I had been chosen from about two hundred and fifty applicants to serve as the "in-house" man for selling this drilling program. What the General Partners didn't know was that I had never sold one unit of a drilling program. It was the only question they didn't ask.

The president of the listed General Partners kicked off the presentation by giving his usual dynamic, magnetic and very effective presentation. The president of the Texas General Partner then followed up with a thoroughly knowledgeable discourse on the exploration business, which had been his entire business life for nearly twenty years. Then it was my turn.

I stood up and said, "Gentlemen; a week ago I was a stockbroker in Miami and now I am supposed to be an expert in drilling programs." This broke the ice and unknotted my stomach enough so that I could get through the presentation.

Now, after being involved in raising over $10 million for various oil companies and especially after having had exposure to nearly a thousand independent oil men in a seminar on oil financing I taught for a couple of years for New York University; I have written this book for investors and potential investors in oil. This book is in response to the question, "How do I make a good investment in oil and gas?"

The first step to making a good investment in oil and gas is avoiding a bad investment—one that never really had a chance to start with. If you have had an unsuccessful investment in oil or know someone who has, then, after reading this book, you will know 90 percent of the reasons why the investment did not succeed. By turning the clarity of 20/20 hindsight into forewarning of what factors make an oil deal a turkey before you ever write a check, you'll avoid an almost sure loser.

To evaluate any investment, you must first understand what the investment is. This involves knowing definition of terms, understanding of what kind of investment it is, and knowing what choices you may have in this type of investment.

Second, you need to evaluate yourself as a potential investor to see if this type of investment is within the parameters that suit your circumstance—businesswise, is it your cup of tea?

Third, you need to feel that you are emotionally suited to this kind of investment. Are you comfortable knowing that your money is committed to this endeavor?

At this juncture, you are ready to begin to ask some questions, not so much to separate the bad deals from the good, but to begin to ascertain which may be the most suitable for your purposes.

Now you need to know what benchmarks will be available in the way of information as your investment progresses, to tell you how it is doing. That is, if you make an investment, what information should you expect to receive?

Finally, it is constructive to know how the leading investors in the field operate.

This book will walk you through all of these steps. It will give a surprising number of ironclad rules which should *never* be violated to avoid an almost sure investment disaster. You will see what to do, the steps to take, what to watch out for and why, and, probably most important, how to do it. Also, provided for you are questionnaires and charts.

The Energy Investment Game for individuals will be oil and gas for at least the next ten years and possibly longer. Developing coal reserves is too lengthy and too expensive a process for most, even substantial investors. Alternate energy sources are just emerging and should be avoided like the plague.

An exhaustive study of alternate energy sources, called *Energy Futures*, carried out for the Congress in 1976, concluded that alternate energy sources (solar, shale, fusion and other technically exotic types) would not be economically feasible until about the turn of the century or until the price of oil reached an equivalent of $45 to $50 per barrel in 1976 dollars. While progress in technology can negate or modify this conclusion, we know that there is huge demand for oil and gas and that there will be in this century. There is a lot of oil and gas still untapped underground. This oil and gas will be proven up by drilling.

Some of you may question the validity of the statistics (often quoted in newspapers and magazines) emanating from the American Petroleum Institute and the American Gas Association as to the existence of substantial untapped reserves. Aren't you a bit more convinced when you read of continuing huge new discoveries in the already exciting Overthrust Belt or the opening up of a totally new area of tremendous reserves (maybe 10 to 20 billion barrels) in places like the Beaufort Sea? Even in shallow, low reserve potential areas like Ohio, drilling activity is at an all time high because oil prices are also at an historical peak.

The oil exploration industry is going to be a big winner over the next twenty five years. If you are a qualified investor, you too, can be a winner—by not being a loser—in this most exciting and potentially profitable game, the Energy Investment Game.

What This Book Will Do For You

- DEMONSTRATE step by step how to avoid "can't win" investments.
- EXPLAIN questions you should ask before consider an offering.
- SPELL OUT the comparative advantages of the forms of business you can invest in.
- SHOW how to maximize tax deductions in oil and gas ventures.
- GIVE ideas for deducting more than you invest this year.
- REVEAL how a typical investment shapes up.
- PRESENT how to size up the odds and stakes.
- SET FORTH formulas for analyzing past performance and future risk of oil and gas ventures.
- OFFER tips on what to look for in an engineering report.
- TELL how some reserve valuations may be pipedreams based on misleading engineering studies.

Contents

1

Skull Session: Learning the Rules of the Game

WHAT IS THE ENERGY INVESTMENT GAME?

The energy investment game is played by about 10,000 oil companies who spend some $16 billion per year to get oil and gas out of the ground and put it in a form of fuel, lubrication or petrochemicals. To do this, they drill about 50,000 wells a year, both onshore and in the offshore waters of the United States.

WHO ARE THE PLAYERS?

The Chase Manhattan Bank of New York is considered one of our leading oil banks and they put out a semi-annual Energy Survey which follows the progress of the oil and gas industry with emphasis on the twenty-nine largest companies. A fully integrated oil company is one which discovers, develops, produces, markets, refines and transports petroleum. Those companies who do all of this are called "majors," and for purposes of this look-see, the twenty-nine followed by the Chase will be the majors.

The rest of the 10,000 oil companies are called the "independents," mainly because they are mostly concerned with discovering, developing and producing oil and gas *independent* of the refining, transportation and marketing functions.

WHERE DOES THE MONEY COME FROM?

Individual investors are playing an increasingly important part in financing the search for oil and gas.

About two-thirds of the $16 billion comes from the 29 majors. They get about two-thirds of their share of expenditures from earnings which they generate from producing oil related products. The rest comes from sources outside their companies, such as borrowings, the sale of securities such as common and preferred stock, and joint venture money from other oil companies. All oil companies invest with other oil companies in order to participate in more wells and spread the risk.

The independents, the other 9,971, spend a third of the total money used to find and produce liquid and gaseous hydrocarbons. They don't have the earning power of the majors, so only about 40 percent of their money comes from internal earnings. The rest comes from the same outside sources, but also includes over $1 billion from outside investors who are not oil companies. These are principally individual investors in SEC registered oil programs. There are no available and reliable figures on how many dollars go into oil investments from non-SEC registered oil deals, but it is probably close to double what is raised in registered security offerings.

It is this estimated $3 billion that this book will be concerned with. Based on the "average" $25,000 investment in SEC registered *drilling* programs that raised $750 million, we can arrive at a figure of over 300,000 individual investors in oil and gas ventures as your prospective fellow players. Add to that the substantial investors in private, unregistered, non-exempt deals and you have a total of roughly 400,000.

HOW DO THE RULES OF THE GAME WORK?

Before we can go on, you need to know the rules of the game—how it works, or at a minimum, how it is supposed to work. If you are familiar with the oil business, this brief section may bore you. If you have made any money in the oil business *without* knowing these fundamentals, then you are like the wife who sat down to play poker for the first time with her husband and some of his buddies. After the first deal she asked, "Are two pair of ones any good?"

Oil people refer to themselves as "being in the oil patch," just as a stockbroker will say he is "in Wall Street." Although Wall Street is literally in lower Manhattan, the oil patch in the United States extends to 33 oil and gas productive states.

"Well" is a loosely used term but should refer to a well that has been drilled or is being drilled.

"Prospect" is the correct way to refer to a well you expect to drill. A prospect has two inseparable elements; a geological idea that beneath the surface there is oil or gas that can be sold at a profit over the cost of the well; and second is the acreage overlying the prospective subsurface target zone which is available for drilling (usually by leasing the drilling rights from the owners). Without available acreage, the geological idea remains only that and without the idea, the acreage remains simply farmland.

What Types of Drilling Are There?

I have heard promoters classify prospective wells, variously, as:

A little wild, but if it hits, it could be a barn burner!

It's a step-out. A little risky, but just over the county line they got lots of wells been producing over 50 barrels a day for fifteen years.

We call it a close-in well. Next to our lease on the Jones Ranch, they got twenty-five good wells.

What these loose descriptions probably refer to are drilling *exploratory, semi-proven* and *proven* prospects, respectively. There is still a lot of debate as to exactly where the line should be drawn between the categories. Most of the valid definitions of these types come from geologists, people who study the earth. As you know, the earth is made up of layers like a cake. Some of these layers have structures which form a trap for oil and gas. The oil or gas is not trapped in a "pool" or a "basin" as we conceive of it on the surface, but rather is contained in the pores of rocks or sands. Super porosity is 20 percent, but you can have good commercial production from one percent porosity. Oil and gas bearing porosity is more prevalent in formations in certain geologic ages than in others.

The first discoveries of oil and gas were almost accidental. There was seepage from the earth. At first, crude oil was used for medicinal purposes. "Snake oil" bottlers noticed that in certain areas seepage was likely to occur, and they sought out these areas to refill their panacea pots. In other words, they found one area analogous to another. After Colonel Drake made his first oil discovery in Titusville, Pennsylvania in 1859, others started punching holes all around.

Then some production was founded in the West. Many early wildcatters found that a lot of successful wells could be drilled around salt domes (a phenomenon you can see from the air today, the main difference being that the dome is now ringed with oil wells. Molten subsurface salt had heaved up through the surface and trapped oil and gas around its periphery.) Others who noted the analogy of salt domes found more oil in other places.

Petroleum geology has become more and more complex and far more accurate than it was with the early salt-dome-seekers, but it is still basically the application of analogy. So, if there is a productive well adjacent to a proposed lease prospect, adjacent being on the nearest permissible acreage unit, then the prospect could probably be called *proven* if the target depth is the same formation which is producing nearby. (Most states have a Department of Natural Resources which spells out how close wells can be drilled to each other without robbing the structure of recoverable oil or gas. This spacing is called a minimum acreage unit.) If production is some distance—probably two or three acreage units—be that unit 40, 80, or 160 acres, it might qualify as *semi-proven* if the well is drilling for the same not-so-nearby productive formation.

Almost any prospect a mile away from proven production from the same formation would qualify as *exploratory*. You can have a wildcat virtually next door to a big proven production if there is a fault in the earth which has made the adjacent acreage non oil-bearing.

The odds against being in on an exploratory well that discovers a major new field (50–100 million barrels) are over 100 to 1. The chances that you'll be in on a discovery of a good commercial field, say a million barrels or 6 billion cubic feet of gas, are about 1 in 25 or 30, depending on who you talk to. Almost all the really big discoveries will be made by the major oil companies who drill horrendously expensive wells—maybe $5–$15 million each in lots of fifty to two or three hundred per company per year. These companies must concentrate on the tremendous reserves needed to replace what they are now producing. For this reason, the majors generally stay away from the smaller deals. Corporate overhead of large oil companies won't let them work the smaller deals, as well. This is a principal reason that about 80 percent of the wells drilled in the United States are drilled by independent oil companies. It is also one of the reasons that an individual investor can get participation in 30 or 40 exploratory wells in a year for no more than $5,000.

Which Type of Drilling Offers the Greater Return?

Proven and semi-proven wells offer less risk than exploratory wells, but they will offer less return. Often these two classifications are lumped together and called "development wells." The principal reason that the return will be less is that proven and semi-proven acreage is, in most cases, owned by an oil company or someone who already owns production. The owners have a good handle on the approximate value of either what is under proven acreage or what is near semi-proven acreage. They also know what the cost of drilling their acreage would be. This gives them some idea of what kind of return on investment can be had so they price the acreage accordingly.

An analogy with plain real estate applies here—a piece of land next to a busy shopping center is more valuable than some land on the edge of town. Adjacent land values are known, rents have been established, and a traffic count is available. The real estate developer who owns the shopping center property might choose to sell rather than spend the money on construction of a building. The owner of proven or semi-proven acreage has the same choice.

Rather than spending more money drilling by himself, he chooses to cash in and sell the acreage to someone else who then drills a development well. The limited return is caused by the higher price which must be paid for the acreage. This brings us to the second step in drilling a well—acquiring the right to drill. In the order of things in the oil patch, first there is a geological idea usually drawn from analogy (or an engineering report from a petroleum engineer). Then someone has to get the right to drill on this acreage.

How About Acreage and Acquisition?

Most oil companies have landmen, whose job it is to seek out desirable acreage to drill on. Others depend on independent lease brokers. Either way, it is the job of the landman to find out and know who owns the drilling right to what acreage and what the going market is.

Leasing acreage on which to drill is quite a business in itself. Oil and gas leases are acquired by two means. First, a cash "bonus" is paid for the right to drill over a limited period of time. Second, the landowner receives a royalty on any production coming from his acreage. If the well is not drilled on the acreage within the time specified by the terms of the lease, it expires unless the landowner is paid an additional delay rental. If production occurs, the acreage is "held by production," that is, by payment of the royalty.

Very often, the royalty is more important than the cash bonus in the case of development wells. A geologist I interviewed on behalf of a prospective investor bragged to me about what a coup he had pulled off in leasing a certain 6,400 acres. He looked at the investor, smirked cannily, and said, "I finally got Rancher Johnson to lease me this acreage. Shell had been after him for ten years, but I finally talked him into it at the same price they'd been offering—50 bucks an acre! Now about this new well being drilled . . ."

"How about the royalty?" I interrupted.

"Oh yeah, he got that, too. Now about this new well . . ."

"What royalty did you give, and what was Shell offering?" I broke in again.

He glared daggers at me and said quickly, "Shell was holding out an eighth, but I went ahead and offered another sixteenth—a really sweet deal. Now about this new well . . ."

When the geologist (who was trying to sell a deal he had put together) left, I explained to the prospective investor that the difference in a one-eighth and a three-sixteenth royalty was the difference between a 12.5 percent royalty and an 18.75 percent royalty. He was then less impressed with the geologist's finesse in wresting the lease away from Shell.

The standard landman's chestnut (probably of 1930 vintage) concerns the two farmers talking over a fence about leasing to an oil company:

> Farmer #1: "Guess you leased your land to that feller from Superoil?"
>
> Farmer #2: "Yup."
>
> Farmer #1: "Guess you got the same price I did, ten dollars an acre?"
>
> Farmer #2: "Yup."
>
> Farmer #1: "Guess you got a fourth royalty, like me?"
>
> Farmer #2: "Hell no, I held out for a sixth!"

There are still a lot of landmen working the countryside and making deals over a cup of coffee in the landowner's kitchen, but this is often in areas that are being ignored by the majors. One thing for sure; all landowners these days keep up with current prices, and both cash bonuses and royalties are increasing continually.

In the big oil plays in highly prospective areas, oil companies have not only acquired satellite maps of the area, but in many cases have put county lease records on a computer. If a good discovery is made, the nearby landowners whose names spew out of the computer, are contacted by phone to negotiate leases. This is done in the manner of a high pressure land or stock sales boiler room, except in reverse; they're buying, not selling.

With these fundamentals under our belts, let's take a look at how an oil company functions.

HOW OIL COMPANIES WORK

Oil companies, whether they be giants of the industry or one man operations, follow these functions unique to the oil industry.

Who Handles Acquiring the Acreage and How Do They Do It?

In a major company, this would be handled by the Land Department, probably with a large staff. In a small firm, there could be one landman. In a very small firm, the services of a lease broker could be used either by simply purchasing acreage through him or by putting him on retainer to give a right of first refusal to acreage in certain areas. A one or two man partnership with some land experience could purchase drilling rights direct from owners.

Acreage to drill on can be acquired in several ways. Land could be purchased in fee simple—that is, the land and all rights that go with it, including the right to drill or mine it under the surface. For oil people, though, unless they intend to farm, graze or develop it, this is prohibitively expensive. When an oil man talks about "buying land" or "buying acreage" he means buying the right to drill on the acreage which is owned by someone else.

The really big leases that you have read about in recent years are the offshore leases controlled by the Federal Government. The prices for these tracts are almost always bid on by the major companies and the largest independents. The prices are so high in the millions that even the big companies join together in consortiums or joint ventures to bid. You have read about the Baltimore Canyon off the coast of New Jersey and the Georgia Embayment off the coast of several southern states. These tracts are offered at auctions by sealed bids from joint venture groups.

Oil and gas productive states usually have a Department of Natural Resources, which among other things, controls the leasing rights to state-owned lands. Acreage rights on these lands are usually held at sealed-bid auctions, like the offshore leases.

Quite common is the acquisition of drilling rights by paying a cash bonus for the right to drill on a certain number of acres for a specified period. If a well or wells are not drilled within the terms of the lease, it expires and to retain the lease would require renegotiating a new lease or paying what is called a delay rental. Landowners always ask for and get a landowners' royalty—a percentage of gross revenues before expenses—on any production from drilling on their land. Cash bonus prices are increasing in most areas, as are royalties.

Not only are cash bonuses and royalties increasing and the time spans of leases getting shorter, but also in some areas where there has been production at shallow depths with good discoveries made more recently down deeper, some landowners are limiting not only the time span, but also the depths to which the well can be drilled. An owner of land which overlays production from several formations at different depths might lease drilling rights down to 6,000 feet to Company A, from 6,000 to 12,000 to Company B, and below 12,000 to Company C. In cases like this, title searches could get to be like playing three-dimensional chess.

If production is made and the landowners receive their royalty, the lease is valid so long as there is production. Most leases require that the well be put into production as soon as is practical so the owners will receive their royalties promptly.

In 1968, one major company bought a dominant acreage position in Michigan which had had some production for some time. They bought literally hundreds of thousands of acres at cash bonuses of some $10 per acre, plus a one-eighth royalty for the right to drill over a ten-year period. The company proceeded to discover and develop the Niagaran Reef play and has produced from it many millions of barrels of oil and billions of cubic feet of gas. Currently, prices on acreage in the vicinity of production are running $110–$125 per acre with royalties running three-sixteenths to seven-thirtyseconds. The major company is having a very difficult time in renegotiating leases that did not get drilled, even at these dramatically higher prices. The reason is that the owners of land that did not get drilled see their neighbors driving Cadillacs bought with production royalties.

What, of course, happened was that the major company bought more acreage than it could afford to drill. The owners of the undrilled acreage are refusing in many cases to re-lease to the major, and in fact, are calling the independents to offer them the same acreage at the same price the major was willing to pay, but for a much shorter period, often two or three years. They want their Cadillac, too!

Most of the major companies have huge acreage positions. The current energy crisis, intensified by the oil companies' capital appetites, have created many opportunities for the independent oil companies. As stated earlier, the majors have chosen (or really been forced) to concentrate their efforts where the big potential reserves are. This is often offshore or much deeper. For several reasons they have been forced to this posture. First, they must replace the reserves they are producing. Secondly, the cost of deep and offshore drilling is almost astronomical. Most likely you have read about offshore lease prices. Once a discovery is made offshore, a platform is usually built to drill development wells. Often one of these platforms may cost $25–$100 million. Thirdly, the overhead of a major oil company usually cannot be supported by a million barrel field.

Many of the majors and larger independents have lots of good acreage that they can foresee that they will not be able to drill. In cases like this, the owner of big acreage could agree to "farm out" the acreage. That is, the owner of the drilling rights would assign these rights to someone else to do the actual drilling in return for a percentage interest in production. The farmout arrangement offers advantages to both parties: it allows the independent to gain drilling rights with no cash outlay *and* it gives the owner the right to some of the future production without any of the cost or risk of drilling.

Are Acreage Acquisitions Made at Random?

Just who guides the choice of where a good prospect may be? In exploratory drilling, this usually involves geologists and/or geophysicists or both.

What You Should Know About Geology

A geologist is one who has knowledge of the earth. A petroleum geologist is one who has—and seeks—knowledge of that part of the earth which may contain oil or gas reserves. A geophysicist is one who studies and knows the physical properties of oil- and gas-bearing subsurface formations and who applies this most often in attempting to correlate information available from the surface with what may be below. There is often an overlap in function between the two fields and a lot of common knowledge.

A geologist may be the salaried employee of an oil company or he may be an independent consultant and almost anything in between. Some are on partial retainers to show a portion of their work to those who pay the retainers. Others are consultants for a fee only. Some put together deals, including acquiring the acreage rights, and sell them for a profit. If they sell their deals to the oil industry, this is called "turning a deal." That is, they are turning the deal over for a profit, some of it in cash up front, but often for a percentage of production if the well is successful.

The acknowledged great in the field of petroleum geology was Dr. Everett DeGolyer, who took time out from school to go to Mexico and help Harry Sinclair make some big discoveries. He founded the firm which bears his name today, DeGolyer and MacNaughton, which is the largest petroleum consulting firm in the world.

Geologists operate by analogy, reduced clues and logic. Before there was an oil industry, the early geologists concluded that the layers of the earth which they could observe in cliffs eroded by wind and water were of a certain age. Archeological and mining work preceding the oil industry confirmed this. As the field of petroleum geology became an accepted natural science—before the turn of the twentieth century—geologists confirmed (by the results of drilling) that certain geological ages tended to produce oil while others did not. I once asked two successful geologists how old the Jurassic Age was, and they argued heatedly as to whether it was 150 or 180 million years! After the argument, each wrote me a letter in support of his hypothesis.

Just how oil and gas originated is something that has not been proven beyond question. It has to do with age and pressure and heat and their effects on certain types of fossils, but no one knows for sure. The largely accepted adage in the oil patch is that "oil is where you find it." I did have one well-qualified geologist tell me that he was absolutely convinced that oil and gas came from prehistoric sharks—no sharks, no oil or gas. Maybe he's right.

The most reliable information a geologist has to work with is information gained from the drilling of wells, whether productive or dry. The negative information gained from drilling a dry hole is valuable, if expensive. Data gathered from wells drilled is referred to as "subsurface control." When a well has been drilled to a certain depth, only then is it known for sure what is down there. When the drill bit drops, the BS stops.

Even very good subsurface control is no guarantee of a successful well, although it is the best assurance available. An "inside location," one which is surrounded on all four sides by production, can be a loser. For instance, there could be a very hard rock formation under the inside location which breaks off drill bits at such a rate that it is not economic to drill.

The geologic ages have built up formations which exhibit certain characteristics. Two extreme examples of formation characteristics would be a comparison of the Niagaran Reef in Michigan with the Clinton Sand in Ohio. The Reef, a crescent shaped formation ringing the northwest corner of the Michigan peninsula, is often quite deep but very narrow. Production from Reef wells is often several hundred barrels per day from a depth of about 7,000 feet. The well must be almost dead on top of the reef to be a good one, because the Reef is so narrow. On the other hand, the Clinton formation in Ohio is almost a blanket formation which underlies a large part of the state at fairly shallow depths. Seldom is a Clinton type well non-productive, but without proper engineering it may not be an economic success.

The next most reliable information a geologist works with is information from the surface, called "surface control." Often a geologist will call in another specialist, a geophysicist, who knows the physical makeup of the subsurface and who is skilled in obtaining geophysical information from the surface. This is information gained sometimes from underground specific gravity, and sometimes from underground magnetic attraction. The two devices to obtain this information are called the gravimeter and the magnetometer. They are generally used for more preliminary investigation of areas which are not productive, or evaluating unplumbed depths.

The most widely used tool for getting surface information on what is below is the seismograph. This is a device which utilizes the bounce of underground sound waves to give an indication of what is underground.

The sound waves are sent below either by an explosive charge or a device called a thumper. The sound waves which are reflected are charted on moving graph paper. The graphs so produced give a "picture" to the geologist of what is underground. Seismic investigation can indicate with surprising accuracy what is several miles beneath the surface. It can indicate a formation and what should be a hydrocarbon bearing structure or trap, but it cannot indicate, alas, the presence of oil or gas. Using the seismograph, the geologist or geophysicist can draw a subsurface contour map to show how the earth is layered below.

Using both surface and subsurface controls when available, the geologist then draws an analogy with other similar areas and concludes that a well should or should not be drilled. Further study and analogy help to determine the exact location of the well on the prospect. Most geologists admit that petroleum geology is almost as much an art as a science, and that intuition can be a large factor in finding oil.

Once oil has been discovered, determining how to maximize the production of the reservoir and calculating how much in reserves may be recovered from the reservoir is generally the bailiwick of the petroleum engineer.

What You Should Know About Petroleum Engineering

The field of petroleum engineering has numerous branches. Of primary interest to investors and potential investors is reservoir engineering. A reservoir engineer is one who has two functions of great interest to investors. In the case of a discovery in exploration, they estimate how much oil or gas may have been discovered, and then calculate how much can be removed or brought to the surface for sale.

In a development (proven or semi-proven) drilling venture, it will probably be an engineer who helps the geologist determine where the wells will be drilled.

To find out how much oil or gas is in a reservoir, the engineer will take the results of a laboratory study of core samples, among other things, brought up by drilling wells. The core sample shows the amount of porosity. The results of drilling will tell about how thick the structure is. The best way to define a reservoir is to drill outward at minimum well spacing until all wells on the periphery are dry. This can be too expensive, though. The rough subsurface shape of the reservoir can be determined as subsequent wells are drilled. That is, the structure may begin to thin out. By taking the thickness of the productive reservoir, a profile can be drawn which approximates the shape of the formation. When it appears to be too thin to support the cost of additional drilling, no further wells are drilled.

Engineers have three initial measurements:

1. *porosity*, which tells how much oil or gas the structure holds per cubic foot;
2. depth or *thickness in feet* (often called "acre-feet of pay"—in mining, they would call this paydirt); and
3. *areal extent.*

By taking the oil or gas bearing porosity and multiplying that total by the acreage involved, the engineer can get a reasonable estimate of how much oil or gas there is under there and arrive at a potential value in place underground. This potential is often expressed in "acre-feet of pay," the thickness of the pay zone, times the acreage overlying it. Multiplying the estimated content (based on porosity) times the acre-feet of pay, times the estimated price of oil gives the number needed.

But oil underground is of no value unless it can be brought to the surface and sold. In order to produce oil or gas, there must be enough *permeability* in the formation for the oil or gas to flow or be pumped to the surface. Permeability in a formation may be enhanced by various means from the surface. Among other things, the formation may be "fractured" by forcing water or sand or other substances under pressure through the formation to help open it up.

An example of zero permeability is oil shale which is so much in the news these days. Oil in shale is contained in the pores of the shale, but it will not flow at all. In order to extract the oil from the shale, the rock must first be crushed and the oil forced out by pressure and high temperatures. This is why shale oil, while plentiful, is very expensive.

Even with good oil bearing porosity and adequate permeability, this still does not tell what the potential value of the oil or gas may be. Oil and gas wells do not produce at a uniform rate. That is, if the life of a given field is ten years, this does not mean that the field will be produced at ten percent per year. Oil and gas production normally shows three recognizable states. First, is the stage of "flush" production, when both pressure and flow are very high. This is usually a relatively short period in the life of the well. Then the well goes through a stabilization period in which both pressure and flow, while declining, do so at a fairly small and relatively predictable rate. The final stage is the "decline" period in which production flow and pressure drop off to a point of making the well marginal. In past years almost any well with small production or in its "decline" period was loosely called a "stripper well," and was marginally economic to produce at $3.00 per barrel. The Energy Act of 1978 defined stripper wells as those producing ten or less barrels per day, and permitted more liberal pricing of their oil than other so-called "old oil." Stripper wells can be economic at the current price of over $42 per barrel.

The decline curve of an oil well generally looks like a bowl tilted on its side or, as they call it in geometry, a hyperbola. Mathematicians say this decline is at an exponential rate.

Charting a future decline curve is a matter of recording both flow and pressure of a productive well for about six months. Then, based on the information gained from actual experience, a projected decline curve may be charted to show an engineering estimate of production potential—how much recoverable oil or gas is down there.

Seldom is an engineering study done on a single well. Usually, at least one "confirmation" well is needed.

Once an estimated production curve has been established, this will give an idea of how much in recoverable reserves are in the field. It is still necessary to "produce the field on paper" in order to arrive at an estimated economic value.

How Is Future Net Revenue
Calculated?

Once estimated gross production has been arrived at, the engineer must project both a selling price for the oil and gas and the cost of production. Selling price times production, less costs, will give projected future net revenues. These must be discounted for the time value of money. That is, a dollar received next year, if the prevailing interest rate is 10 percent, is worth only 91¢ compared with a dollar received today. With this discount, you then have the present rate of future net revenues.

Petroleum engineering is dealing with an asset sometimes miles down in the ground and many contingencies can arise which can change this picture. For this reason, most experienced engineering firms use a further discount of 30–40 percent to allow for unforeseen risks.

The resulting estimate is the present worth of future net revenues discounted for both the time value of money and risk. This is a figure used as a benchmark for the sale in place of petroleum reserves, and gives a good idea of what the field is worth at the present.

In order to calculate future net revenue, the engineer prepares a *Prospect Analysis*. A sample can be found below. This analysis is an estimate of recoverable barrels of oil (BBLS) and thousand cubic feet of gas (MCF). (For time value of money and risk discounting to provide for present worth see Chapter 2.)

PROSPECT ANALYSIS

Date: March 2, 1980

State   WYOMING   County   MAJOR
Prospect   #2424-6   Location   SE/4-20-10N-13W
Prospect Name   JOHNSON
Classification   DEVELOPMENT   Prospect;   LOW   Risk
(Possible Reserves Assuming Successful Average Completion)

Primary Zone   RED FORK   TD 7,700'   Secondary Zone
  Future Gross Production   Future Gross Production
    Oil, Bbls.   Oil, Bbls.
    Gas, MCF   Gas, MCF
    GOR   GOR

	Before Payout	After Payout	Total
Future Gross Prod., Oil, Bbls.			75,000
Future Gross Prod., Gas, MCF			112,500
Working Interest			.250
Net Interest			.186075
Future Net Prod., Oil, Bbls.			13,956
Future Net Prod., Gas, MCF			20,933
Unit Price after Severance:			
Oil, $/Bbl.			11.625
Gas, $/MCF			1.6275
Future Gross Revenue, $:			
From Oil			162,239
From Gas			34,068
Total			196,307
Operating Cost, $ (10%)			19,631
Gen. & Adm., $ (5%)			9,816
Cap. Expense & W.O., $			0
Ad Valorem Tax, $ (0%)			0
Future Net Revenue, $			166,860
Initial Investment, $			99,725
Gross Return on Initial Investment			1.7 to 1—pre tax

Recommendations: PARTICIPATE

Payout Calcs	Program Cost	Client Only Cost
Land and seismic, (gross: 0) × (client - %) equals		0
Drilling (gross: 81,725) × (client - %) equals		76,150
Completions (gross: 62,575) × (client - %) equals		(99,725)

Management Fee
Total Cost
Unit price oil   11.625   Gas   1.6275   GOR   1.5
Composite   14.066   Net   2.617
Adjusted for GA, OPN, AVT   15-85
8/8ths units to PO   % Total   44,826

Notes:
1. Above estimates assume a successful completion at indicated location. 2. Assume program owns ½ of   interest, client pays all of program's share of intangibles. 3. Rights only to base of Red Fork. 4. Client risk—$96,725. 5. 160 acres. 6. Estimated payout: two years.

Now, which function comes first, acreage acquisition, geology or engineering? The answer is "yes!" That is, an oil operation can start at any phase of the cycle. It could be with a land-oriented person who knows of, has, or has access to some prospective acreage; it could be a geologist with some ideas that need to be drilled up; it might be with an engineer who has a proven prospect which needs backing. In a full-sized oil company, all three functions are interdependent.

In any oil operation, all three phases are dependent upon money. Some of this money will likely come from investors like yourself, and that's why you're reading this book—to gain information. But information is not enough. You need to find if you qualify as an investor in oil and gas ventures, and then how you can invest.

2

Can Anybody Play?

No! Nor should many investors who have—often to their chagrin and economic suffering. By the same token, there are still many investors shunning investment in oil because of second hand tales of woe they have heard from unhappy investors, many of whom should not have been putting their money into oil in the first place. Here is a brief history with some comments on how oil financing has evolved over the past century.

A THUMBNAIL HISTORY OF EARLY OIL FINANCING

The bulk of oil financing during the first seventy years of the oil industry's life was done just the opposite of the way porcupines make love—with wild abandonment. There was no regulation of any consequence as to how an oil man or oil company could raise money until the creation of the Securities and Exchange Commission in 1933.

Prior to the creation of the SEC, oil and gas exploration was financed by five primary means. First, a few very wealthy individuals invested in

33

single and multiple well deals. Second, syndicates were formed, composed of some wealthy individuals who wanted to participate in drilling activities. Thirdly, the banks helped in financing the oil business by making loans. Then, within the oil industry itself, both majors and independents invested in each others' deals by taking partial interests and thereby spreading the risk over a larger number of wells. Finally, both majors and independents financed significant amounts of exploration and development from earnings and other internally generated funds.

The creation of the SEC, over the long term, instead of ruining Wall Street as the financiers of the thirties feared, brought Wall Street to Main Street, although it took a while. Wall Street, the brokerage community, did not market long-term bonds for oil companies until Mr. Sinclair went to Wall Street in the thirties and sold them on the validity of using this investment medium. Common stock financing still plays an important role in oil company financing.

Direct investment in oil through the brokerage community was not made widely available until the late 1960s. Probably the primary reason for this was the lack of a suitable form in which to offer to the investing public direct participation in drilling oil and gas wells.

Until the 1960s, almost all direct investment in oil and gas ventures was done through either general partnerships or joint ventures. Let's take a look at the characteristics of these two forms of business and then compare the qualities of the limited partnership.

FORM VERSUS SUBSTANCE

How you invest can be almost as important as *what* you invest in certain businesses. The continual capital appetite of the oil business makes it one of those in which form is very important, in addition to legal liabilities attendant.

How General Partnership Works

A General Partnership entitles each partner to share the profits of that partnership in ratio to his interest in that partnership. In addition, each partner is liable for his share of obligations. In general partnership, if you had made what you thought was a $50,000 investment and the majority of the partnership decided to require another $50,000 investment and you did not have it, then your interest could be diluted. Of even greater concern is the legal liability of a general partnership. Each partner is liable for his share of legal liabilities to the extent of his net worth. If some catastrophe struck which created a judgment against the partnership which took all the net worth of all your other partners, then the claimant could invade your net worth. Disaster insurance can be purchased, but it is not economical to fully insure most high risk ventures. This open-ended liability is not very palatable to most individual investors.

How a Joint Venture Works

A joint venture is one in which each participant shares profits and losses to the extent of his interest. Liabilities are shared jointly and so from a practical standpoint, joint venturers of approximately equal net worth stood to lose equally if things did not go well. This is the form that the numerical majority of oil ventures take today. Most oil companies joint venture with one another.

Both the general partnership and the joint venture have in common a community of management. That is, the group would go along with the majority (if the papers were drawn that way) and each partner or joint venturer had a say-so in managing the business. The partner who chose not to go along with an extra capital contribution would suffer dilution of his interest. Most oil joint ventures, recognizing that a successful discovery will require additional funds for development, impose a penalty for not making additional contributions. Joint venturers sign documents to authorize additional expenditures called "authorities for expenditures," called "AFE" for short. Most joint ventures are drawn to impose a penalty for non-consent to AFE's for additional funds.

Since successful development of a good discovery may depend on far more money than the original investment, it becomes vital that the additional money be there. For this reason, most oil oriented joint ventures have heavy penalties for "going non-consent" or not signing the AFE. Most oil companies and large investors are delighted to consent to additional assessment for completion of a successful exploratory well or the development of a field discovered by a wildcat well. They also have the money to meet substantial assessments of this nature and size. Most individuals are not financially able to subject themselves to this open-ended obligation.

By heavy penalty, I mean that a typical oil joint venturer who chose not to consent to an additional $100,000 expenditure might be subject to a "300 percent penalty for non-consent." This means that a non-consenting joint venturer would forfeit, in this case, $300,000 (300 percent of the $100,000 additional he did not put up) in future production revenues attributable to his share of the venture before he would even begin to get his money back.

How a Limited
Partnership Works

A limited partnership has two classes of partners, the general partners and the limited partners. Usually there are one or two general partners and several limited partners.

The limited partner gives up all management say-so in the partnership to the general partner(s). In return for total management of the enterprise, the general partner guarantees that the limited partners will have no liability beyond his original investment. This form of business solves the double potential problems in the general partnership and in the joint venture of both financial and legal liability being without limit.

Bear in mind that the general partner's guarantee against liability can only be as strong as his net worth, but the limited partnership form is used by almost all oil offerings involving either an exemption from registration or a full registration with the SEC.

The limited partnership was not widely available until the late 1960s when the Uniform Limited Partnership Act was adopted by all the states. It then became feasible to market an oil offering on a widespread basis in compliance with both state and Federal securities laws.

The chart below may be of assistance in understanding how various facets of the type of organization may affect certain aspects of investor ownership. This is not a legal study but merely a practical survey of how these forms are supposed to work if properly written and carried out.

Forms of Business

From the Individual Investor's Point of View	General Partnership	Joint Venture	Limited Partnership	Corporation*
Losses	Flow Through To Investor	Flow Through To Investor	Flow Through To Investor	Do not flow through to investor. Future earnings, if any, can be sheltered to the extent of these losses.
Legal Liability	Full—Up to Your Future Net Worth	Theoretically Limited to Your Percentage; Possible Full Exposure	None	Normally None
Financial Liability (Assessments & Commitments)	Full—Up To Your Future Net Worth	Theoretically Limited to Your Percentage; Possible Full Exposure	No liability beyond original investment	Normally None
Debt Financing	Recourse to Individuals Unless Assets of Partnership Can Collateralize	Same as General Partnership	Normally Non-recourse and only if Management (G.P.) is Authorized to Borrow	Normally Non-recourse to Stockholders
New Equity Capital Investors	Must Form New Partnership	Usually Form New Joint	Must Form New Partnership	With Stockholder approval the corporation may sell new shares at any time
Taxes	No tax paid by partnership if all earnings are distributed to partners, who will pay individual taxes	Same as General Partnership	Same as General Partnership	Income taxed at corporate rate; if distributed, taxed again as dividend
Liquidity	Usually None	Usually None	Highly Restricted; Usually None for Practical Purposes	Free Transferability
Transfer of Partial Interest	Usually Reform Partnership	Usually Reform Joint Venture	With Management's Permission; Must Refile Partnership Papers	Free Transferability

* Not including Subchapter S; Assumption that shares are issued as "fully paid and non assessible shares" and that stockholders have pre-emptive rights.

SECURITIES REGULATIONS AND THE OIL INVESTOR

The Securities and Exchange Commission was created and the Securities Act of 1933 was written to provide uniform investor protections. One of the main thrusts of the Act of 1933 is to provide "full and fair disclosure" to potential investors in the form of a uniform offering document, the prospectus.

The use of the limited partnership form for all sorts of non-stock-and-bond financings led to an expanded concept of what a "security" was. Here is what the courts came up with:

- A pooling of funds
- In the expectation of making profits
- From the efforts of a third party, constitutes an *investment contract.*

By this definition, a couple of people who invest with an operator in an oil deal have created an investment contract. They have bought a security, a piece of paper that says they own an interest in an oil deal.

Does this mean that almost all oil deals offered to investors fall within the jurisdiction of the securities regulators? Probably.

Does this mean that most oil deals are financed either by a valid exemption from registration or by full SEC registration? Not by a long shot. The fact is that the vast majority of oil deals are financed in at least theoretical contravention of securities regulations.

The Oil and Gas Journal in May of 1978 reported the results of a survey of over 1,100 active oil operators who had drilled in excess of 20,000 wells over a twenty-year period. The survey asked how many of these operators had utilized two of the most used exemptions from registration, Rule 146 and Schedule D (which will be discussed later in this chapter). Only 15 percent answered in the affirmative. This means that many oil offerings do not provide the full and fair disclosure required by the Act of 1933—in many cases the investors are not only *not* getting the full story, they may be getting the full treatment.

The figures from the above survey are not meant to imply that 85 percent of oil deals are fraudulent, because the Act of 1933 did provide exemptions from registration. For instance, intra-industry joint ventures would not need to come under these regulations because there is a presumption of sophistication and foreknowledge that the non-oil industry investor does not have.

In addition, the Act of 1933 provided a valid exemption for private placements. Among the private placements, exemptions and full registration, here are the choices of form that a potential investor in oil faces in 1980.

WHAT YOU SHOULD WATCH OUT FOR WHEN DECIDING WHICH OFFERING TO CHOOSE

Private Placements

The private placement grew out of an exemption in the Act of 1933 provided by Section 4(2). This section exempted from registration with the SEC, "transactions by an issuer not involving any public offering." Most valid private placements today are joint ventures among industry investors (like the consortiums who invest in offshore leases) or sometimes among non-industry corporations who want to get into the oil and gas business to get the oil and gas to use.

There are many groups of substantial investors who have invested in oil ventures on a private placement basis. They are usually in the oil business or very close to it. They are normally wealthy, have a lot of experience in oil and gas investment, know each other, and know the principals in the operation very well. About the only way a novice investor gets invited into a private placement is on a promoted basis. That is, one of the participants sells (or offers you) a piece of his action at a markup. Stay away from private placements.

Rule 146 Exemption

Rule 146 spelled out guidelines for interpreting the intent of the Section 4(2) exemption and placed strict limitations on its use. This came about in 1974. The effect of the Rule 146 exemption was to make it less expensive for smaller deals to be marketed on a highly restricted basis. Since 1974 there have been thousands of Rule 146 offerings, both fraudulent and valid. It is usually less expensive for the smaller issuers and since the costs of offering are often charged to the investors, it has resulted in less cost up front to them.

How Do You Recognize An Invalid 146 Offering?

See if it follows the rules. The first rule of the 146 exemption provides that any number of offers can be made to previously qualified investors. This means that the investors should have substantial net worth and income and have sufficient business experience and knowledge to make an informed business judgment as to the suitability of the investment for their own portfolio.

For their own protection, all valid issuers of 146 exemptions should require that an investor fill out a *suitability questionnaire before* giving him an offering memorandum. This is usually a one page document which asks your net worth (usually without home, furnishings and automobiles) and taxable income. It asks you to affirm that you are sophisticated in investments. Your filling this out shows that the issuer has "previously qualified" you. If you are not asked to fill out such a questionnaire before you receive an offering document, don't even look at the offering. The issuer is not playing by the rules. If he skips this one, he'll skip others and you don't want to waste your time even looking at the deal.

For your convenience, provided in the following pages is a sample *suitability questionnaire.*

CONFIDENTIAL

BROKER/DEALER'S PRELIMINARY OFFEREE
SUITABILITY QUESTIONNAIRE

(To be completed prior to delivery or showing a
Memorandum to a Prospective Offeree)

INSTRUCTIONS TO PARTICIPATING BROKER/DEALERS

SINCE LTD., (THE "PARTNERSHIP") IS
A PRIVATE PLACEMENT, THE PROCEDURES FOR DEALING
WITH POTENTIAL OFFEREES ARE RATHER STRINGENT
AND MUST BE STRICTLY ADHERED TO. ACCORDINGLY,
YOU ARE REQUIRED TO COMPLETE THIS QUES-
TIONNAIRE PRIOR TO DISCUSSION ANY OF THE FEATURES
OF THE OFFERING WITH ANY PROSPECTIVE OFFEREE.
This Questionnaire should be filled out by the Broker/Dealer's repre-
sentative and not by the Prospective offeree. Please immediately
transmit this complete Questionnaire to   LTD.

The purpose of this Questionnaire is to provide the Partnership
with preliminary information on the suitability and sophistication of
a prospective offeree. Only when the Broker/Dealer's representative
is reasonably satisfied, as a result of the answers obtained, that the
prospective offeree will probably meet the suitability and sophistication tests described in the Confidential Investment Memorandum
dated February 1, 1980 (the "Memorandum"), can a Memorandum
be delivered.

1. Prospective Offeree's name:————————————
2. Address: ————————————————————

————————————————————

3. Estimated annual income for 1979: $———————————

4. The estimated annual income of the prospective offeree for 1979 meets the requirements recited in the Memorandum.

☐ YES   ☐ NO

5. Estimated net worth: $_____

6. The net worth of the prospective offeree is reasonably believed to be substantial, i.e., equal to or in excess of the net worth requirements cited in the Memorandum.

☐ YES   ☐ NO

7. Statement of prospective offeree's sophistication:

_____

_____

_____

8. The prospective offeree is reasonably believed to be capable of bearing the economic risk of an investment in the Partnership:

☐ YES   ☐ NO

9. Does the prospective offeree have a pre-existing relationship with your firm?

☐ YES   ☐ NO

10. Will the prospective offeree retain or otherwise have available the services of an Offeree Representative?

☐ YES   ☐ NO

11. Do you have reason to believe the prospective offeree (along with the Offeree's Representative) is(are) suitable in light of all relevant circumstances?

☐ YES   ☐ NO

Date Memorandum Delivered:_____

Memorandum No. _____ Delivered

Broker/Dealer Firm Name

Registered Representative or Principal
(Print or Type)

Signature of Registered Representative
or Principal

Branch Office Address

Date this Questionnaire Signed

ALL INFORMATION WILL BE TREATED CONFIDENTIALLY

LTD.

OFFEREE SUITABILITY QUESTIONNAIRE

Gentlemen:

The information contained herein is being furnished to you in order for you to determine whether the undersigned's Subscription Application to purchase Limited Partnership Interests (the "Interests") LTD., (the "Partnership"), may be accepted by you pursuant to Section 4(2) of the Securities Act of 1933 (the "Act") and Rule 146 promulgated thereunder ("Rule 146"). The under-signed understands that (A) you will rely upon the information contained herein for purposes of such determination, (B) the Interests will not be registered under the Act in reliance upon the exemption from registration afforded by Section 4(2) of the Act and Rule 146.

In accordance with the foregoing, the following representations and information are hereby made:

I. (This item is presented in alternative form. Please initial, in the box provided, the alternative you select).

☐ ALTERNATIVE ONE: The undersigned has knowledge and experience in financial and business matters so as to be capable of evaluating the relative merits and risks of an investment in the Interests; the undersigned is not utilizing an offeree representative in connection with evaluating such merits and risks. The undersigned offers as evidence of knowledge and experience in these matters the information requested below on this Offeree Questionnaire.

☐ ALTERNATIVE TWO°: The undersigned under-stands that you may require using the services of an offeree representative(s) (as defined in Rule 146) acceptable to you ("Offeree Representative") in connection herewith. The undersigned acknowledges the following person(s) to be such Offeree Representative(s) in connection with evaluating the merits and risks of an investment in the Interests:

(List name(s) of Offeree Representative(s)):

_____

_____

The above named Offeree Representative(s) has(ve) furnished to the undersigned a completed Offeree Representative's Questionnaire, a copy of which is delivered to you herewith. The undersigned and the above-named Offeree Representative(s) together have such knowledge and experience in financial and business matters that they are capable of evaluating the merits and risks of an investment in the Interests.

IF YOU HAVE INITIALED ALTERNATIVE TWO, THIS OFFEREE QUESTIONNAIRE *MUST* BE ACCOMPANIED BY A COMPLETED AND SIGNED OFFEREE REPRESENTATIVE'S QUESTIONNAIRE.

II. The undersigned is willing and able to bear the economic risk of an investment in the Interests in an amount equal to the total subscription amount. In making this statement, consideration has been given to whether the undersigned could afford to hold the Interests for an indefinite period and whether, at this time, the undersigned could afford a complete loss. The undersigned offers as evidence of ability to bear the economic risk, the information below on this Offeree Questionnaire.

III. Except as indicated below, any purchase of the Interests will be solely for the account of the undersigned, and not for the account of any other person or with a view to any resale, fractionalization, division, or distribution thereof.

(State "No Exceptions" or set forth exceptions and give details. Attach additional pages if necessary)

_____

_____

_____

Except as indicated below, any purchase of the Interests will be solely for the account of the undersigned, and not for the account of any other person or with a view to any resale, fractionalization, division, or distribution thereof.

(State "No Exceptions" or set forth exceptions and give details. Attach additional pages if necessary)

_____

_____

_____

_____

The undersigned represents to you that (a) the information contained herein is complete and accurate and may be relied upon by you and (b) the undersigned will notify you immediately of any material change in any of such information occuring prior to the closing, if any, with respect to the purchase of Interests by the undersigned.

INFORMATION REQUIRED OF EACH PROSPECTIVE OFFEREE

1. Name: _____ Age:_____

2. Residence Address and Telephone Number:_____

_____

3. Employer or Business Association and Position:_____

_____

4. Business Address and Telephone Number:_____

_____

5. Business or professional education and the degrees received are as follows:

School	Degree	Year Received

6. Prior employments, positions or occupations during the past five years (and the inclusive dates of each) are as follows:

Employment, Position or Occupation	Nature of Responsibility	From	To

Attach additional pages if necessary to answer any questions fully.

7. (a) Gross income during 1979: $_____

   (b) Taxable income during 1979: $_____

   (c) The highest tax rate at which federal income taxes were paid during 1979 _____ %

8. (a) Estimated gross income during 1980: $_____

(b) Estimated taxable income during 1980: $_____

(c) Estimated highest tax rate at which federal income taxes will be paid during 1980: _____ %

9. (a) Estimated net worth (exclusive of residence, furnishing and personal automobiles):

$_____

(b) Liquid assets are as follows:_____

_____

_____

(c) Non-liquid assets are as follows:_____

_____

_____

10. (a) Tax shelter investments to date are as follows:

Nature of Investment	Tax Losses Reported on Tax Returns to Date

Attach additional pages if necessary to answer any questions fully.

11. (a) During 1980 anticipated losses from tax shelter investments are as follows:

Nature of Investment	Anticipated Tax Losses for 1980

_____

_____

_____

12. Investments in oil and gas programs during the past five years are as follows:

Nature of Property   Amount Invested

_____

_____

_____

_____

_____

_____

13. The undersigned has previously purchased securities which were sold in reliance on the private offering exemption from registration under the Securities Act of 1933:

_____ YES   _____ NO

Attach additional pages if necessary to answer any questions fully.

14. During the past five years additional investments in real estate limited partnerships, not set forth elsewhere in this Questionnaire, have been acquired as follows:

Year   Investment

_____

_____

_____

_____

IN WITNESS HEREOF, I have executed this Offeree Questionnaire this _____ day of _____, 198 .

_____

Signature of Prospective Investor

_____

Print Investor Name

Attach additional pages if necessary to answer any questions fully.

PERSONAL FINANCIAL STATEMENT OF

who resides at

as of   1980

Assets

  Cash in Banks
  Notes and Loans Receivables
  Marketable Securities
  Commercial Real Estate
  Personal Real Estate°
  Equity in Private Businesses
  Other (Describe°°)

  Total Assets   ―――――――

Liabilities

  Notes and Loans Payable
  Mortgages Payable°
  Other (Describe)   ―――――――

Total Liabilities   ―――――――
NET WORTH   ―――――――

Annual Salary   ―――――――

Annual Other Income   ―――――――

1976 Taxable Income   ―――――――

――――――――――――――――

Signature

Provide in addition:

  1. Name of Bank:
  2. Detail on any asset in excess of $100,000 or 25% of net worth.

―――――――――

° Do not include home.
°° Do not include automobiles or home furnishings.

51

Next, the manner of solicitation is limited not only to those people who have been previously qualified, but the number of takers is limited to 35. (While most Rule 146 offerings are limited to 35 investors, additional investors who commit $150,000 or more may be included without violating the normal numerical limitation.) The manner of solicitation restriction means avoiding any aspect of a public offering. That means no advertisements in newspapers, periodicals or on the electronic media. A popular means of getting exposure to phony 146 offerings is to place ads in newspapers advertising "Information on Tax Shelters" and giving an inward WATS-800-number to call for information. What you get when you call the WATS number is a sales pitch on some oil deal, and not information on tax shelters.

The same has been done with direct mail. An impressive letterhead stands atop the stationery. A drilling rig takes up the left hand margin. There is then a brief pitch about the energy crisis, how oil prices have increased 800 percent since 1973, and what a super inflation hedge reserves in the ground are. (It's also patriotic to invest in oil, but they usually don't mention this.) All of this is true. Then you are given a telephone number to call for information on how YOU, TOO, CAN TAKE ADVANTAGE OF DIRECT INVESTMENT IN THE FUTURE OF THE ENERGY IN-DUSTRY!!!! Don't waste the phone call.

Is there anything you can do if you have been talked into an invalid (or even fraudulent) offering? Yes! You may ask that your money be given back. If this does not work, you may sue the promoter/general partner/sponsor in exercise of your right to rescind your commitment. This right is generally made on the basis that "you were sold an unregistered security" and/or that you "did not have access to the same information which you would have had if the offering had been fully registered."

You do not have the right of rescision just because results have been disappointing economically. But, if in the opinion of a qualified attorney, the offering is not a properly drawn Rule 146 exemption and if the document does not give full and fair disclosure, it may be worth your while to ask for your money back. Often an unscrupulous promoter will give back the money rather than risk exposure. On the other hand, an honest promoter will spend more than you have invested to protect his good name and you may have to spend more than your investment in legal fees in a fruitless suit.

The same right may apply to improper intrastate offerings. There is a comment on these under the Intrastate Exemption section of this chapter.

Rule 146 requires disclosure of "all relevant" information. Most securities attorneys agree that this means that, in a Rule 146 exemption, the investors should get the same information that he would get if the offering were fully registered with the SEC. Now, strangely enough, no offering document is required. However, the burden of proof (if there is ever any question by an investor) is on the issuer.

The only way an issuer can prove that you got information on the offering is to give you a numbered copy of the offering document (they should always be numbered so the issuer can limit and control the number of copies) which you have to acknowledge receiving by your signature. If the vendor of a purported 146 gives you a document without asking for your signature, throw it in the trash. You might not know about the previous qualification questionnaire, but you now know about both it and signing for the offering memorandum. Don't even read the cover if you are not asked to sign in advance.

Now for the offering document itself. These come in a variety of forms. The most elaborate are bound volumes in leatherette-like material, sometimes gold-embossed and labelled, "Confidential Memorandum." This is often a red flag, though not infallibly. A too-fancy offering document means that probably the issuer is making an inordinate profit and can spend money on useless window-dressing like this. Or it means the investors will be charged for this on completion of the offering. Others come in 8½″ × 11″ paperback, like a thick manual. Some are spiral bound. Often, they are offset-printed typewritten booklets and there is nothing wrong with this. Setting type is very expensive and is not required by the 146 guidelines.

A ten minute scanning of the document will indicate in large measure whether this is a scam or if the purpose of the document is to give the potential qualified investor information. If there are extensive typographical errors, misspellings and generally sloppy appearances, the odds are large that this sheaf of papers was designed to help transfer your dollars to the issuer's pocket, and leave a minimum of bucks in the deal itself. It is likely that the reason that the issuer has not taken time to proofread the document is that he's operating out of his hip-pocket, from a rented furnished office and a post office box. Also, his time is taken up with packing a fresh bag every day so he can get out of town on short notice if someone blows the whistle on him.

You should know now that the securities regulators are not looking for trouble. They are available to check out investor complaints. If they do not get complaints, they do not investigate or attempt to enforce. They are not like the FBI, out looking for violators. They are available to assist investors who feel they have a complaint. The best protection the unscrupulous oil promoter has is that an investor will feel too sheepish at having been taken to complain.

So far, little of this chapter has told you much about oil investment itself. The reason is that if you get into an investment which was not designed to profit anyone except the issuer or promoter, then you don't need to know anything about oil. You can draw a blank in a chinchilla farm or gold mine deal just as easily as in an oil deal—and without any study at all. If you can avoid the patently deceiving deal, then you have paid for this book many times over the first time you don't get taken.

The above has stressed not so much the negative aspects of the 146 exemption, but those signs which steer you away from them if you heed them.

You Should Also Weigh the Advantages of Rule 146

The positive aspects of the Rule 146 offering are several. First, it is less expensive to make such an offering than to go through a full SEC registration, especially if the sponsor sells it without going through a broker. It does require a larger initial investment than an SEC registration because of the limitation on number of investors to 35. Few valid 146 offerings are made in the oil business which require less than a $25,000 investment. If it is less than this, you should question it seriously. The reason for this is that unless the deal proposes to drill fairly shallow wells, it cannot offer much diversification. A single well deal is a poor crap-shoot, if you are not in the industry.

Most 146 offerings are self-limiting as to the net worth and income of the investors. The majority of them follow guidelines set forth by certain regulatory bodies (the states and a voluntary self-policing body in the brokerage community called the National Association of Securities Dealers.) These guidelines usually call for a minimum net worth of

$200,000 *or* a net worth of $100,000, and some portion of your income taxed at 50 percent. The net worth requirement usually excludes home, furnishings and automobiles. If you do not comfortably qualify, do not even consider trying to get into a 146.

Another plus of the 146 is that it can have staged payments, that is, several payments over a period of years. From the oil operator's standpoint, this is a big plus because it usually takes more than a year to complete and develop discoveries.

A final plus in most 146 offerings is that they often describe the prospects to be drilled. That is, if it is a five well deal, then the details of the five wells are included in the offering document. This would allow a potential investor to give this information to a geologist or an engineer and get a professional evaluation before investing. The reason that the 146 can include specified properties and a full SEC registration usually cannot, is the time required for processing the SEC registration through to the issuance of a full and final prospectus. This takes about six months normally, and may take a year. It is not good business practice to pay for a lease you know you won't drill for six months to a year. A 146 document can be written in four to six weeks, so specified properties are usually a feature.

There is one other area of regulation you should know about and that is the state securities regulations. After the formation of the SEC, the states began forming their own securities regulatory agencies. All 50 states have some type of anti-fraud or securities regulation, generally referred to as "Blue Sky" laws. Even though the 146 has exemption from Federal regulation, the deal must be qualified for sale in the states in which it is offered— offered, not just sold. (Connecticut is the sole exception.) As a reminder, if you were recently cajoled into a 146 and you are not happy with it and the sponsor did not qualify by registration or exemption in your state, you probably can get your money back by exercising your right of rescission.

Schedule D Exemption

The Schedule D exemption was originally intended to make very inexpensive, very small oil offerings. It is limited to $250,000, and cannot offer adequate diversification. A Schedule D must be a joint venture, with open-ended financial and legal liabilities. Because a very small amount of money is involved, the Schedule D exemption has been the most abused of all the exemptions to the extent that numerous states will not even qualify a Schedule D for sale to its residents.

An exception to this almost blanket condemnation of Schedule D offering is in Ohio. The State of Ohio requires that offerings to Ohio residents only be made via a Schedule D questionnaire which an attorney can fill out for sometimes under a thousand dollars, so any promoter can play. Stay away from Schedule D offerings and save yourself a needless economic loss in most cases.

Intrastate Exemptions

It was mentioned briefly earlier that the Act of 1933 provided an exemption for offerings to residents of a single state. Many of these states have statutory limitations which permit investment by a limited number of bona fide residents of that state to invest in a domestically domiciled organization with fairly minimal disclosure requirements. The limitation on number of investors is often accompanied by a requirement that a certain portion of the money be invested in the state in which it is offered. This limitation on use of proceeds almost automatically disqualifies the use of an intrastate exemption in the 17 non-oil or gas producing states.

In the oil productive states, the restrictions imposed by the state regulatory authorities often impose limitations that make the intrastate exemption too small in dollars to provide adequate diversification. In most cases, intrastate oil offerings should be avoided.

SEC Registered Drilling and Development Programs

The SEC registered oil and gas offering did not come into wide usage until the passage by all fifty states of the Uniform Limited Partnership Act in the late 1960s. This provided the brokerage community with the vehicle necessary to offer to many smaller investors direct participation in oil and gas ventures but without the open-ended financial and legal liability involved outside the limited partnership.

The oil and gas operating community at large looked sneeringly at the early SEC registered drilling programs. Most oil men felt that the expense involved in setting up such an offering was too great for them. They felt that the work involved was onerous. With increasing Federal regulation, many felt they did not want to add another Federal Agency (the SEC) to the list they were already dealing with. The oil people pointed out that the cost of offering was usually passed on to the investor, which took away from economic potential. Finally, they normally went to great lengths to point out that from their point of view that the "drilling funds" were a good dumping ground for deals they couldn't sell elsewhere.

Despite the alleged investor objection in 1970, 89 sponsors raised $291 million via registered oil programs.

With all this lack of enthusiasm by the host industry, how did the registered drilling programs manage to raise almost 10 percent of the nation's cost of finding, developing and producing oil and gas?

Basic economics provided much of the impetus. In 1970, domestic oil was selling for under $3 per barrel. The posted price then for natural gas was 15–17¢ per thousand cubic feet. These selling prices were getting perilously close to the cost of finding, developing and producing these commodities. The prices of oil and gas were (and still are) regulated by a Federal agency, the Federal Power Commission (now the Federal Energy Regulatory Commission). Return on investment in the oil industry was so low that in 1971, drilling activity dropped to a 10 year low. It was clear within the industry that prices had to escalate or a substitute had to be found—the one that makes present economic sense has not shown up yet, though it may someday come. The then-FPC was aware of this, and price increases were cautiously granted until the Arab oil embargo of 1973 sped up this process. Higher prices came as the industry knew it would, but with a sudden rush instead of an ordered rise.

A second reason for the early success of SEC registered drilling programs was the internal condition of Wall Street. The brokerage business had suffered a triple blood bath in the 1968–1970 triennial. Problem A in Wall Street was that the great bull market which had surged upward since World War II from under 200 on the Dow Jones Average to over 1,000 had ended. The market, which was supposed to go up because it always had, stopped doing so.

Problem B was the inability of the brokerage industry to process the paperwork of the volume generated by the tail end of the bull market.

Problem C for Wall Street was its own capital crisis. The huge volume generated by the bull market, coupled with the inability to process trades on a timely basis (with attendant snafu of major proportions in record keeping) strained the capital of some even major Wall Street firms to the point of bankruptcy.

By 1970, over 100 of the some 800 New York Exchange Member Firms had either merged or folded up. Those remaining were faced with increasing investor disenchantment with, and declining volume of, common stocks and stock-based mutual funds. It was necessary for the survivors to seek out not only additional products which could be widely marketed by their branch offices, but also products which had a relatively high profit margin.

A third reason for the popularity of the SEC'd oil offerings was the Tax Reform Act of 1969. Among other things, the 1969 Reform Act took away or modified many of the benefits of most tax incentive investments. The 1969 Act modified the tax advantages or investment in oil and gas only to the extent that it reduced the allowance for oil and gas depletion from production revenues from 27.5 percent to 22 percent. It left untouched the primary tax incentive for getting into oil and gas initially—the intangible drilling cost deduction, which allowed most of the costs of drilling a well (whether dry or productive) to be deducted as a business expense from income from other sources.

A late 1969 edition of *The Institutional Investor,* a magazine widely read by Wall Street professionals, featured the drilling programs in an article entitled *Oil Programs—Gusher on Wall Street?*

Unfortunately, the many criticisms of the public drilling programs from within the oil industry itself seemed to have been valid in the wake of the bankruptcy of three major sponsors of widely marketed drilling programs in the early 1970s. The first had been an eminently successful marketer whose main internal problem was that it raised more money than it could prudently drill up—they drilled a lot of marginal wells simply to provide the promised tax deduction. The other two were frankly frauds, as reported in the Wall Street Journal. They either took excessive fees which were deposited in foreign banks, or they simply drilled "paper wells." That is, they reported drilling many non-existent wells and simply pocketed the money.

Wall Street was somewhat to blame for some of these problems. First, by and large, the brokerage community was not so sophisticated in oil and gas investment as it is now. It was not in a position to monitor on behalf of its investors, the staff of an operating company and make a valid judgment as to whether the staff was large enough to administer the kind of money Wall Street was capable of raising.

Second, many Wall Street firms did not do a really thorough job of preliminary study of the firms whose programs they sold. This is called a "due diligence study" and entails a comprehensive effort by the under-writer or marketer of securities to ascertain that what they are offering to their investors is exactly what it purports to be. Wall Street, in its haste to diversify into popular oil programs, in many instances did only preliminary investigation into oil programs' sponsors.

The SEC itself, was not prepared for the "gusher on Wall Street" in 1970. The information required of the drilling program sponsors was not nearly so precisely defined, nor so meaningful within the oil industry as the information presented to a potential investor in 1980.

The problems of some sponsors in 1970 who left in their wake some unhappy investors, have created a better investment atmosphere for investors in direct participation in oil and gas in 1980. The SEC has beefed up its personnel handling oil and gas offerings and has separate forms especially designed for such offerings. Most Wall Street firms now have on their staff either former petroleum engineers or geologists to assist them in their due diligence efforts on behalf of prospective investors. Most Wall Street firms use outside consultants, as well, and perform continuing monitoring services of drilling programs on an ongoing basis. In the wake of the foregoing negative remarks of the potential weak points of drilling program investment, let's take a look at what the potential investor in registered oil and gas programs in 1980 has to choose from.

1980 PROFILE OF AN SEC REGISTERED DRILLING PROGRAM

Since we are still concerned with form rather than substance, let's break down major points of the "product" you may be considering investing in. First, consider what the cost of the product is and second, take a look at what you are getting for these costs.

Investor Costs, Front End, Ongoing and Backend

Front end costs include the commission paid to your broker, the cost of registration and offering (mostly legal expense to attorneys for writing the prospectus, and the cost of printing it). If there is a non-recurring "management fee" the first year, this, or part of it at least, may be considered front end cost. Selling commissions will range from 6.5 percent to 8 percent, with some few programs giving a discount for large orders in the form of allowing the retail broker to negotiate downward for large orders. There are often other marketing expenses, such as maintaining a force of "wholesalers" or a dealer-manager group whose job it is to educate brokers and make presentations to groups or to individuals on behalf of brokers.

Front end charges may either be charged directly to the investors by deducting the amounts from the proceeds of the offering, or they may be advanced by the sponsor in the form of a loan or a straight advance to be recovered from some portion of production.

The total front end charges for registered drilling programs in 1979 ranged from 11.75 percent to over 20 percent. It is interesting to note that in 1970 the range of front end costs of SEC registered programs was 12.5 percent to over 25 percent. In 1970 the majority of registered programs charged over 18 percent in front end costs. In 1979 the majority of programs took about 14 percent off the front end. Competition for investors' money has sharpened the pencils of most sponsors.

The nature of the non-recurring management fees may or may not include them in front end fees. If the management fee is a pure, non-risk profit for the sponsor, then it should be called a front end charge, especially if it is in addition to either another fee or reimbursement for overhead and administrative costs.

If the management fee is in lieu of overhead and administrative charges and is limited to the amount that can be allocated to the particular program, then it could be included as an initial portion of ongoing fees.

Ongoing fees may be of two types: those which are charged for running the partnership, and those which are charged for specific functions. An ongoing fee of the first type would be for the purpose of administering the partnership, including keeping books, communicating with investors, reporting to the SEC and IRS, with some portion allocated to covering office and field overhead costs. These usually cost from one to three percent of funds originally raised, and recur annually. An ongoing fee of the second type would be for the purpose of operating producing wells and monitoring their production.

Where ongoing fees for specific services become objectionable is not the instance in which they pay for the work actually done, but when they amount to paying the sponsor for monitoring the efforts of someone else *who is also paid by the partnership.* In this instance, the fee becomes a double dip for the sponsor. By and large, competition among the SEC registered programs doesn't let this happen very often. It is rarely seen anymore, except in a newer program which usually modifies this very quickly.

Back end fees are a bit more difficult to explain and fall into the structure and substance which are discussed more in depth in Chapter 4. For our general purposes now, back end fees (or profits) are those interests which accrue to the sponsor, usually in excess of his investment, if any. Some back end fees are cushioned by providing that they may not be paid until the investor has gotten all his money back first—the term is "payout," but how it is defined may be very important to the economic success of the venture. A more detailed comment will be made later on both payout definition and various forms of back end fees and profits.

What You Should Get for What You Pay

The SEC registered drilling program is more expensive to acquire than the typical Rule 146 exemption, and much more expensive than most private placements which usually do not have an offering document. The biggest part of front end is the retail commission paid to the broker who sells it, about seven to eight percent of the total money invested.

This commission doesn't all go to the broker in the branch office. He gets to keep a portion, often less than half. The balance goes to the brokerage firm's main office to cover the expenses of due diligence studies and to give some cushion against the liability of an underwriter. Some of the problems of the early SEC registrations were blamed on lack of adequate due diligence studies by the vending brokers. This is no longer the case. When the broker agrees to handle an SEC registered drilling program, it is only after his firm has investigated the sponsor, his staff, and the program itself, as if the firm were going to buy the offering *in toto*, itself. The largest vendor of drilling programs says it spends at least $30,000 in time and money in each due diligence study.

The due diligence study differs markedly from the information in the prospectus in that there is a lot more of it sought. The brokerage firm wants to know not only if the offering involves full disclosure, but also if it has the potential of being a good investment for clients.

The brokerage firm will hire experts of all manner to go through the office and operations of a drilling program sponsor. These experts would include accountants, attorneys, landmen active in the proposed areas of interest, geological and geophysical consultants, engineers and sometimes, even private detectives to check out the backgrounds of individuals.

Once the muster of a due diligence study has been passed by a drilling program, then the brokerage firm spends time, along with the drilling program sponsor, in educating the broker salesmen of the firm as to what kind of offering it is. And from this educational effort comes another part of the benefit you should get when you buy an SEC registered program—a basic education from the broker who handles your account.

If your broker suggests that you consider buying a drilling program, he will be prepared to sit down and explain it at length to you. An acceptable alternative is that he may ask an associate in his office who specializes in tax incentive investments to explain it to you. If you have not read a drilling program prospectus before, it will likely take you four to eight hours to digest what you read in the first one. A knowledgeable broker can explain most programs in about half an hour.

If you digest this book carefully, you will know within fifteen minutes if your broker is knowledgeable and if he has done his homework. You've paid for this benefit—take advantage of it.

The second largest front end cost is in the form of legal fees to ha e the prospectus written, followed by the costs of having it printed. Attorney's fees for writing a prospectus for a drilling program will range from about $35,000 up to about $150,000. The investor usually ends up paying this fee and for it he gets standardized information which is scrutinized by both the SEC and the state authorities for full and fair disclosure.

The amount of research needed to write a prospectus for a registered drilling program is extensive. It includes not only the latest information on securities laws, but also updates on legislation affecting the oil and gas business, farily lengthy comments on partnership law, and the latest on tax legislation affecting oil and gas investments. In addition, the prospectus may include one or more legal opinions by the attorneys, who charge for the potential liability of having rendered this opinion.

A lot of the verbiage in prospectuses is what is called "boilerplate," that is, standard information and wording which will apply to nearly any similar offering. With some practice, you can learn to spot the boilerplate and dig into the heart of the offering very quickly, but it will take some study and comparison.

The sponsor of a drilling program, the general partner, takes the initial risk of the cost of offering because if it doesn't clear the SEC, if the underwriter withdraws for any reason, or if the deal simply cannot be sold, the legal and printing bills end up on the sponsors' desk. This means that an oil operator who plans to offer an SEC registered program should be substantial and have a good record, or he is unduly risking his money. I saw one SEC registration in 1978 which had been put out by a sponsor whose only business experience had been in real estate. He spent $80,000 to have an offering registered with the SEC only to find that, much credit to both brokers and investors, investors are not going to buy an oil deal from a real estate man—and they shouldn't.

Perhaps it's the "grass is always greener" syndrome which is part of the human condition, but I should tell you that in 1972, I saw a registered real estate deal sponsored by a successful oil man which did not fly, either. All this is by way of saying that an investor in an SEC registered oil offering should expect experienced management.

In every prospectus, there will be extensive information about not only the operating company, but also the individuals who run the company. Since this is the key to any successful business, you must have this or your money would be better employed elsewhere. Nearly every year, there are a few new names which are offered in the way of SEC registered programs by new companies.

In each such new program prospectus, you will see the caveat repeated to the effect that "since the operating company has no history (or a very short one) of operating such a drilling program, that there is no assurance that the management will be successful." In the case just quoted from above, the three principals had over one hundred years cumulative experience working for other firms in the oil patch before they consolidated their efforts formed their company two years earlier. In a case like this, it is fair to assume that simply banding together did not negate their century's experience—but the fact *was* disclosed.

Perhaps the greatest benefit to the average oil investor in the 1980s is the amount of diversification offered in an SEC registered drilling program by the pooling of money by many limited partners.

Another benefit realized by investors in SEC registered programs generally is excellent continuing communications. The ongoing fees charged help pay for a staff member or an outside specialist to provide these communications. Most SEC'd programs provide monthly reports to the limited partners during the period of active drilling. By and large, these reports are translated from the jargon of the oil patch into reasonably plain English. The communications of the SEC registered programs are generally far superior to those provided to private placement investors, and are well worth what they cost.

A final plus to most registered drilling programs is that often they do offer at least nominal liquidity. This is a feature that you should never plan to call on, but in extenuating circumstance, may have some value. A small piece of a limited partnership which has numerous percentage interests in several wells is not a readily negotiable piece of paper. While the property of a partnership can be liquidated as a whole, in most cases, oil investors in even successful programs should consider themselves "locked in" and be content to take production revenues. Many of the oil programs, while recognizing the unmarketable nature of most oil limited partnership interests, do have a provision for repurchase of the interest after a period of time.

A "typical" liquidity provision in an SEC registered program provides that after three years (enough time to develop properties and have a history of production) an engineering study will be made in which proven reserves, along with a projected cash flow, will be provided. Based on the engineering study, the sponsor may offer to buy back the limited partner's interest at the value of proven reserves after two discounts.

The future value of cash flow from proven reserves will be discounted at one to two percent over the then prime rate at a major bank. This value will usually be further discounted 30 to 40 percent to cushion the risk of evaluating assets in the ground.

This is the figure at which the interest may be repurchased. In these days of high interest rates, the discount factors will reduce cash liquidation value to less than half the ultimate value cash flow from future production revenues. Investors realize this to the extent that less than ten percent of investors in programs offering a liquidation privilege (also called a "right of presentment") actually exercise these privileges. If there is the slightest possibility that liquidation might be required in the future, you might want to reconsider investing at this time. It is good to have this right in the case of estate settlement, for instance, but it should not be purchased with liquidation in mind.

The back end costs, touched on very lightly earlier, are the carrot which set the whole SEC'd offering in motion in the first place. Most back end costs are not in the form of cash profits, but are a percentage of production. Usually, this percentage is higher than the investment of the sponsor, if any investment is involved. If no investment were involved, the percentage of revenues going to the sponsor should be realized only after the investors have been fully reimbursed for their costs. This is why sponsors take the risk and extra expense and effort of an SEC registration—to get (or better said, earn) a piece of the pie so big that the only proper way to bake it is through an SEC registration.

Why You Should Avoid Single Well Offerings

Successful investment in oil and gas is a long-term numbers game. Investment in a single well on a one-shot basis is only for the highly sophisticated investor who will probably buy five or ten such deals per year for years at a stretch. Any person other than this who goes into a single well deal is financially suicidal. AVOID SINGLE WELL OFFERINGS!

The best way to do this initially, is to buy an SEC registered program. Of the registered offerings made in 1979, none purported to offer fewer than ten to fifteen well participation. Admittedly, some do not put a specific number in the prospectus (if they raised more money than anticipated, it could prevent their further diversifying). But the drilling program sponsors know they have to provide a return to the investor and to do this they need wide participation in a number of wells. Even the smaller drilling program sponsors with limited staff provide diversification by selling off pieces of deals they originate "in-house", and by buying pieces of others' deals. As a result, for only $5,000, the investor in a registered drilling program gets exposure to a number of prospects which would not be available except in this form for many times that amount. Some oil men object to diversifying to the degree that the registered programs do, saying that if a really big discovery is made, the successful discovery is diluted by diversification. You should be willing to assume the risk!

THE REFEREE MAKES SOME PRE-GAME JUDGMENTS

Now that you have in mind a description of the variety of offerings technically available, here is my objective advice to you as to how you should view them. Next, you will have to make the subjective judgment as to whether or not investment in oil and gas ventures is the right move for you. Here are my calls:

☐ *Private Placements:* First off, probably unavailable to you except on a promoted basis. Usually involves a lot of money with open-ended assessments. This is the bailiwick of the very wealthy, experienced oil investor who is usually in the oil business or connected with it. If one turns up on your doorstep, don't pick it up.

☐ *Schedule D and Intrastate Offerings:* Not recommended. The $250,000 limitation on the amount of money which can be raised via a Schedule D exemption does not permit adequate diversification. The limitation on number of investors (and often the amount of money which can be raised) makes the intrastate exemption generally unappealing. In addition, most intrastate exemptions require that the bulk of funds raised be employed within the state, which makes this type of exemption unavailable in the 17 non-oil and gas producing states. This also limits geographical diversification.

☐ *Rule 146 Exemptions:* Until you have had three years or more of oil investment experience or unless your needs for tax deductions are so large that your tax attorney or CPA recommends a large oil investment, don't put $25,000 or more into a 146. After three years' experience, you may want to consider a 146. If you are ready now, the questions and answers in Chapter 5 will assist you in evaluating the offering.

☐ *SEC Registered Offerings:* This is the game for all first-time investors in oil and gas, and for the numerical majority who invest regularly in legally offered oil and gas ventures. If you are qualified financially and emotionally to put some money into oil and gas, the more than 60 offerings made in the past year should give you the opportunity you are looking for. Now you must make the judgment as to your own qualification to play the Energy Investment Game.

What Are The Usual Financial Criteria?

All the Rule 146 offerings and all SEC registered programs will have minimum financial criteria for potential investors. If you do not comfortably meet these, defer investment in oil and gas until you do.

Most 146 exemptions require that the investor have a net worth (exclusive of home, furnishings and automobiles) of $200,000 *or* a net worth of $100,000 *and* an income that is taxed for Federal Income Tax purposes at 50 percent or more. In addition, you will be asked to represent that you are sophisticated in risky investments and have sufficient business knowledge to make an informed business judgment as to the merit of this oil investment in your portfolio. No matter what you might be tempted to answer in writing on the investor qualification questionnaire, if you cannot say "yes" to yourself without reservation, then pass on the 146, and look for a registered program that suits your needs.

Most SEC registered programs have the same net-worth-only requirement as the typical 146 above, but will permit investment with a net worth (once again, without home, furnishings and autos) of $50,000 and some income taxed at 50 percent. Unless your worth falls comfortably above these figures, you should not get into oil.

You should also be certain in your own mind that you have adequate liquid assets so that your investment in oil will not result in your being strapped in any way during the first three years that your oil investment will be totally illiquid. After that time, liquidity may only be nominal, as explained earlier. You may want to consult with your tax attorney or accountant and get his imprimatur on your proposed investment if you normally consult with him on your investments. Now you must make a self-judgment as to your emotional disposition toward oil and gas investment.

Consider the Emotional Criteria

Oil investment should be part of a long-term program of continuing investment in an industry in which demand will outstrip supply in the United States. It is an industry in which prices will continue to rise for a very basic reason: we now import 45 percent of our oil needs. The OPEC suppliers, with the exception of Saudi Arabia, have a median per capita income of $1,000 or less per year, versus our $10,000 median income.

The $10,000 you put into an SEC registered oil program this year is not going to make you rich. But if you put that amount in every year for ten or twenty years, then as oil prices continue to rise you will have an opportunity to accumulate reserves in the ground which will be producing a large return on investment. How large a return?

At *today's prices*, in a development drilling program (drilling on proven acreage where there are proven reserves), the expected return should be at least $1.50 for each dollar invested. In an exploratory drilling program, the expected return should be $3.00 for every dollar invested. Now these are not cash-out-next-year returns but cash flow from production revenues over the productive life of properties. If the prospects don't have this kind of potential, they probably should not be drilled.

As a guideline, a two for one return for a ten year period is the equivalent of a 7.2 percent return—not terribly exciting until you take into consideration that the oil business has every prospect of higher pricing into the next century. In addition, there are tax incentives which will be covered in the next chapter. That's the potentially bright side of the coin. Let's turn it over.

Are you prepared for disappointing results over the short term if your oil investment doesn't produce as you expected? Do you have the emotional staying power to put some of your money into oil even though the past year looked less than satisfying? If you put yourself in the position of having exposure to a high-potential-return exploratory program, will you be able to continue investing if in one year not enough oil is discovered to even get your money back? If your answers to the above questions are in the affirmative, then you should keep reading. The next chapter covers tax incentives for investing in oil and gas which can make a good investment even better.

3

Please Pass the Shoulder Pads, Uncle Sam

The tax laws of the United States provide tax incentives for many industries. The purpose of tax incentives is to encourage the program for which the incentive is offered. Probably the most widely enjoyed tax break by individuals is the deduction of the cost of interest on a home mortgage. The home building industry would not disappear without this deduction, but home ownership would not be nearly so attractive a proposition.

All the extraction industries enjoy some tax incentives. The industry most in the headlines in the seventies, of course, has been the oil and gas industry. When Congress was debating restricting some of the incentives granted to oil and gas prior to the passage of the Tax Reform Act of 1969, the major oil companies were polled as to how they felt about reducing the then 27.5% depletion allowance to 22%. Their reply was, "If this happens, plan on paying 50¢ per gallon for gasoline." (Premium gas was selling for about 36¢ then.) The depletion allowance was reduced by the 1969 Act and gas did go up to about 48¢.

Tax incentives are still available to oil and gas investment for several reasons. First, to cushion the risk of seeking new reserves—there is no protection from monetary loss but a cushion, like shoulder pads for the football player. This cushion helps to attract capital, too. About two-thirds of our energy comes from oil and gas, so it is obviously an essential industry. Second, like most of the other extraction industries, oil and gas are non-regenerative assets. They can be replaced only by other reserves discovered by more drilling. The depletion allowance for oil and gas is still available to the small producer, although it is decreasing. It provides some non-taxable cash income to set aside for replacement of the diminishing reserves. Hopefully, our legislators are coming to realize that reducing tax incentives has resulted in higher prices at the gas pump.

TAX INCENTIVES AVAILABLE TO OIL AND GAS INVESTORS

Currently Deductible:
Intangible Drilling Costs

The most important initial deduction available to oil and gas investors is the "intangible drilling and development cost deduction." Since 1913, the Internal Revenue Code Section 263(c) has provided that most of the initial costs of drilling an oil or gas well constitute a business tax deduction against other income. What are the "intangibles" of drilling a well?

The major costs of drilling which are deductible as intangible are the drilling rig rental costs, the wages of the drilling crew, supplies to do the drilling, fuel to power the rig, and site preparation costs. These are available whether or not the well is ever productive.

When a prospect has been drilled to its target depth, unless it is clear that there is not any oil or gas (as, for instance, evidenced by a steady flow of salt water which often occurs in what should be oil and gas bearing formations), the well is subjected to numerous tests to indicate whether or not it should be completed. Even if the oil or gas is under natural pressure to come out, this is controlled before production occurs by the use of a substance called drilling "mud." Mud is a liquid whose viscosity and weight are controlled by mixing various substances with liquids at the surface. It has several purposes. First, it circulates around the drill bit to help keep the bit cool and lubricated. It also brings up to the surface the cuttings from drilling. It can be weighted to equalize underground pressures (not only from oil or gas, but often water pressure).

In order to produce the well through production tubing, it is usually necessary to sink protective production casing to keep the hole from caving in and to prevent damage to the tubing from water and other extraneous matter.

Before making the decision to sink the casing, an operator will perform numerous tests to aid in making the decision as to completion or abandonment of the well. The test most often made is the *drill stem test,*[*] in which production is simulated by the equivalent of putting an inflation needle in a football or basketball to see how fast the air comes out. A second test is taking an actual core sample to a laboratory for analysis. Other tests are various forms of "logging." A logging device is a scientific instrument which indicates the presence of oil or gas and can show how thick the formation is.

Example Showing The Effects Of Front End Benefits
For A Married Couple Filing Jointly
(Principally for intangible drilling cost deductions)

Following is a copy of Schedule Y of taxes as included with Form 1040. This is the tax table for married taxpayers filing jointly.

This illustration will show the effect of an oil investment on a married couple with taxable income of $109,000 in both 1980 and 1981. The oil investment will be $20,000 and will provide a 70 percent ($14,000) deduction in 1980 and a 20 percent ($4,000) deduction in 1981.

---

[*] *Drill stem test*—A test conducted during drilling operations to determine the presence of oil or gas in a formation by use of a special tool which is lowered into the hole and removed after contents of the formation have flowed into it for examination.

Married Taxpayers Filing Jointly and Surviving Spouses (§164)

Taxable Income	Tax on Column 1	% on Excess
$ 3,200 or less	$ 0	14
4,200	140	15
5,200	290	16
6,200	450	17
7,200	620	19
11,200	1,380	22
15,200	2,260	25
19,200	3,260	28
23,200	4,380	32
27,200	5,660	36
31,200	7,100	39
35,200	8,660	42
39,200	10,340	45
43,200	12,140	48
47,200	14,060	50
55,200	18,060	53
67,200	24,420	55
79,200	31,020	58
91,200	37,980	60
103,200	45,180	62
123,200	57,580	64
143,200	70,380	66
163,200	83,580	68
183,200	97,180	69
203,200	110,980	70

This couple's base tax on $109,000 taxable income is $45,180 plus 62 percent of the excess of $109,000 over $103,200, or .62 × $5,800. .62 × $5,800 = $3,956. The *tax burden* is $45,180 + $3,956 or *$48,756.* 1980 without tax shelter looks like this:

Taxable income	$109,000
Tax burden	48,756
Spendable income	$ 51,244

Reduction of taxable income by $14,000 intangible drilling cost deduction in 1980 to $95,000 gives a *tax burden* of *$40,870* based on Schedule Y computation. With this deduction, 1980 will look this way:

Taxable income	$109,000
Tax burden	40,870
New spendable income before preference tax	$ 58,130

. Since the intangible drilling cost is an item of tax preference and also since it exceeds the allowable $10,000 exemption, $4,000 will be subjected to the minimum tax for preference items of 15 percent. .15 × $4,000 = $600, so the tax burden after sheltering will increase (and tax savings will correspondingly *decrease*) by this amount.

Here is how to calculate 1980 tax savings:

Tax burden without shelter	$48,756
Tax burden with shelter	40,870
Gross tax savings	7,886
Less preference tax	−600
Net 1980 tax savings	$ 7,286

This net tax savings for 1980 reduces the cost of your investment from $20,000—what you actually paid—to $12,714. The reduction is due entirely to the tax savings, $7,286, which went into the oil program instead of to the IRS.

In 1981, the deduction of an additional $4,000 reduces taxes by $2,570 by the same computations, using Schedule Y once again. Now here is how your investment will stand after these tax savings:

$20,000 oil program investment cost		$20,000
1980 tax savings	$7,286	
1981 tax savings	2,570	
Net tax savings	$9,856	− 9,856
Out of pocket cost of investment		$10,144

While no one can accurately predict the outcome of a particular oil investment, the effect of cost reduction on the return of *any* investment is to increase the return in inverse proportion. That is to say, by reducing the cost of investment by almost one-half, the potential return is doubled.

Depreciation of Capital Completion Costs

A decision to complete a well is a point in time called "the casing point" and it is important to you for two reasons. The decision to sink casing means the initial tests indicate that the well should be a producer. Second, most of the costs from the cost of the protective casing through completion are capital costs. Unlike the intangible costs, these capital costs must be amortized over a period of time and do not constitute a current tax deduction as expenses.

There is an investment tax credit for the purchase of capital goods, but this is not a major item for most individual investors.

The cost of leasing acreage is a capital cost and must be amortized over the life of the well if it is successful. Only if the acreage is abandoned does the lease cost become a deduction.

Depletion Allowance

The depletion allowance, reduced from 27½ percent to 22 percent by the Tax Reform Act of 1969 was eliminated for all but small producers by the Tax Reduction Act of 1975. The "small producer" exemption is generally available to investors in oil and gas drilling partnerships. A small producer is one who has less than 1,000 barrels (or 6,000 mcf feet—6 mmcf of natural gas) of daily production. The depletion allowance for 1980 is still 22 percent of gross income, but may not exceed 50 percent of net income. Under the terms of the 1975 Tax Reduction Act, the depletion allowance will be reduced further as follows:

      1981—20 percent
      1982—18 percent
      1983—16 percent
      1984 and after—15 percent.

The depletion allowance for any one year, even for a small producer, may not exceed 65 percent of taxable income for any one year. If it does, it is carried forward to later years. This is not a problem for most small producer-investors yet.

Here is how the depletion allowance could benefit the investor in a successful oil drilling venture:

If the production revenues attributable to the $10,000 drilling program are $1,500, probably the cost of production will be about a third, leaving $1,000 in taxable income. In 1980, $330 of the $1,000 is sheltered by the depletion allowance and the remaining $680 is taxable.

POTENTIAL DEDUCTION REDUCTIONS—THE TAX REFORM ACTS OF 1969, 1976 AND THE REVENUE ACT OF 1978

One of the avowed purposes of the 1969 Tax Reform Act was to make it almost impossible for a very wealthy person to pay no Federal Income Tax at all. One of the ways this was done was to identify eight items, called "items of tax preference." Included among the items of tax preference were accelerated (faster than straight line) depreciation on real estate and the oil and gas depletion allowance. To the extent that these items of tax preference exceeded $15,000, the 1969 Act imposed an additional tax of 10 percent.

The 1976 Act expanded the number of tax preference items to include the intangible drilling cost deduction. As well, it provided that to the extent that the total of these items exceeded $10,000, the additional tax would be 15 percent, up from 10 percent. (Intangibles were not a preference item for corporations other than Sub S corporations.)

If you own any real estate which utilizes accelerated depreciation, you are aware of the minimum tax on items of tax preference. You also know that if you sell real property on which you had been taking accelerated depreciation before a specified holding period (generally 16 years and 8 months) that some portion of that accelerated depreciation would come back in the form of "recapture"; that is, it would have to be reported as ordinary income on sale and not as a capital gain.

Finally, a blanket proscription against deducting more than the amount of capital at risk was imposed on most all investments with the exception of real estate. That is, 100 percent of your investment is the maximum permissible deduction. This was called the "at risk" limitation, which simply says you cannot deduct more than the cash invested in any one year, or the amount of capital "at risk." It is still possible to obtain valid deductions in one year which exceed the cash invested in that year. While this is a risky proposition, how it can be done will be explained later in this chapter.

The Revenue Act of 1978 made the intangible drilling cost deduction an item of recapture on resale (with some few exceptions) without limitation of time. This reduced the attraction of selling productive properties for a capital gain.

In summary, are the tax benefits of oil and gas sufficient reason to get into this investment? ABSOLUTELY NOT! You can realize the same tax benefit initially from making a charitable contribution—100 percent. If you are not going into oil and gas investment in the long term pursuit of economic gain, you are making a poor investment, and your intent is erroneous.

TWO EARLY POTENTIAL STUMBLING BLOCKS AND
HOW TO DEAL WITH THEM

When the Game is Called Off
Before the Starting Whistle

Every year about a half dozen new SEC registered drilling programs never get off the ground. The reason for this is that most sponsors put in the prospectus a minimum amount of dollars needed to activate the program, say a million dollars. Without this minimum amount, they could not provide adequate diversification. If less than the minimum is raised, the terms of the offering are that all money will be returned and there will be no offering. If you have decided to get into a program that never gets off the ground, you will not have any deductions.

The reasons such an offering fails to sell are numerous: Perhaps the underwriter was inexperienced and overestimated the size of his clients' buying power. An unexpected recession might appear deeper than anticipated and create more desire in investors for liquidity than gain or tax savings. Or perhaps it is just an unattractive program. You would be well advised to consider only those programs with the demonstrated ability to raise the minimum needed to activate.

There is no way of knowing how many proposed Rule 146 offerings never are activated, particularly those which are a first time offering by an oil operator without an underwriter. The best assurance you can have that the offering will be closed is the record of past offerings of the sponsor. If several offerings have met or exceeded the minimum in the recent past, he is likely to be able to repeat the performance.

Partnership Offsides—
Touchdown on Opening Kick
Recalled

Here is another possible pitfall which has nothing to do with the oil business, but has everything to do with getting your tax deductions which is usually the major benefit you will get in your first year in an oil venture. This is not particularly a problem in SEC registrations, but in my opinion is present in about twenty percent of the proposed Rule 146 offerings I have reviewed in recent years.

The reason for discussing the form of business of oil offerings earlier was to give an outline of the advantages of the limited partnership form. It has the protection of the corporate form in that it offers a limitation of liability. Unlike most corporations, the limited partnership allows the losses and gains to flow through to the individual partners based on their percentage ownership. This occurs only if the limited partnership is valid.

Probably because of the tremendous proliferation of tax incentive offerings made in the early seventies, the IRS issued Revenue Procedure 72-13 in 1972. At that time, registered limited partnership oil offerings were raising over a quarter of a billion dollars and real estate based offerings were probably raising two or three times that amount.

The IRS position in Revenue Procedure 72-13 seemed to be that it had no objection to the limited partnership form so long as it was a valid limited partnership.

The Revenue Procedure spelled out net worth requirements for the Corporate General Partner and defined four major characteristics of a corporation. If the net worth—called "safe harbor"—requirements were not met by the General Partner, OR if a "predominance" of corporate characteristics prevailed, then the IRS could (and has) ruled the partnership "an association taxable as a corporation." If the entity is ruled a corporation, then any losses and gains may not flow through to the investors. In the case of first year losses, they could only be used to butt against gains in the event of a successful program. Further, if the program were successful, after the initial losses had been used up, other earnings would be subjected to corporate taxes and, if distributed to the investors, once again taxable as dividends, not a desirable state of affairs.

The "safe harbor" guidelines stated by Revenue Procedure 72-13 require maintenance of the general partners' net worth at the following levels, depending on the amount subscribed:

Amount Subscribed	General Partner's Net Worth Requirement
Up to $2,500,000	$250,000 or 15% of amount subscribed, whichever is less
Over $2,500,000	10% of amount subscribed

The four major corporate characteristics defined are:

1. Continuity of life—corporations theoretically go on forever.
2. Limitation of liability—if you'll notice, most stock certificates contain the description "fully paid and non-assessable shares."
3. Centralization of management—not a community of management like a joint venture or a general partnership.
4. Freedom of transferability of ownership—you can sell shares of stock any time if you can find a buyer.

How the partnership papers are drawn is important. They should specifically spell out why, under the guidelines of Revenue Procedure 72-13, the partnership does *not* exhibit a predominance of major corporate characteristics. How is this done? In layman's terms:

> Limit continuity of life by a termination date—say the partnership will terminate in the year 2010 or 2020. State that the general partner will expose himself to unlimited liability on behalf of the partnership. Severely restrict the transfer of ownership of partnership interests.

This leaves centralization of management, which is a fact. If any limited partner attempts to take part in management, this could also invalidate the form of business. This is usually avoided by having the limited partner sign a power of attorney, giving the general partner the right to perform any function spelled out in the partnership papers without consulting the limited partners—a further protection.

As stated earlier, this is not so much a problem with the SEC registered programs whose attorneys are experienced not only in securities and oil and gas law, but also are aware of the problems of IRS interpretations of partnership validity. This is not to belittle attorneys who draw up Rule 146 exemptions, but I have seen too many of these purported offerings in recent years which had little more than a label, "This is a limited partnership" in both the offering document and in the partnership papers. If you dress a 137 pound weakling in a football uniform and hang a sign around his neck reading "Vicious linebacker," who's kidding whom? I have often questioned whether the poorly written Rule 146 exemptions were even written by an attorney.

Advance IRS Ruling or Opinion of Counsel

There is never any assurance that tax laws will not change or that the IRS may not interpret them differently. It is possible, however, to request that the IRS review in advance the partnership papers and render an advance ruling. The ruling will be hedged very carefully ("under current tax law, it appears at this time") and will state that this is no assurance that at a later date the validity of the limited partnership will not come under further scrutiny nor is there any assurance that the entity will not be taxed as a corporation. IRS advance rulings take about six months to process, which just about parallels the time needed to effect an SEC registration. Most advance rulings you will see will be in connection with an SEC'd offering. Increasingly, though, SEC registrations rely on the opinion of counsel as to the validity of the partnership.

One of the advantages of the Rule 146 exemption is that it can be made more quickly than going the SEC route. For this reason, seldom does a 146 contain an advance ruling, usually an opinion of counsel. If there is any question about the strength of the opinion of counsel, submit the opinion to your tax attorney for his comment.

The President's Tax Message in January, 1978, proposed that all new limited partnerships (except those engaged in housing activities) with more than fifteen partners be taxed as corporations. So far, this has not been made into law, but there is always the possibility that such will happen. The best assurance that you can have is that seldom has major tax legislation been made retroactive.

The first part of this chapter has covered general background on the tax benefits available to investors in oil and gas. You have learned of two potential stumbling blocks to getting these oil and gas oriented deductions. Now, take a look at how you may maximize these tax benefits by taking full advantage of the tax laws as they are currently on the books.

HOW TO MAXIMIZE TAX DEDUCTIONS IN OIL AND GAS VENTURES

Although it is not recommended that tax considerations be the total reason for investing in oil and gas, there are numerous investors who prefer to maximize tax benefits.

Maximizing tax benefits is a matter of trading off, by means of structure of the program, some of the later economic benefits for earlier, but larger, tax deductions. Whether this is the best program for you to follow should be decided in consultation with your tax attorney or accountant.

Here is a checklist of what deductions are available to whom and on what basis. They are given in the order in which they will occur in a typical drilling program sold through a brokerage firm:

- ☐ Sales commission—This is not a currently deductible item. It can be used to increase the cost basis for computing gain on sale of the property.
- ☐ Cost of registration and offering ("syndication expenses")—The legal cost of preparing an offering document and printing it are a small but controversial item. A cautious tax counselor would probably advise against making it a current deduction. Some portion of organization expense may be sometimes be amortized over a five year period.
- ☐ Management fee and/or reimbursement for overhead and administrative expenses—To the extent that these constitute the ordinary and necessary costs of doing business, these are current deductions. *Caution:* a management fee whose primary purpose is paying the sales commission would likely be disallowed upon audit; that is, if the sales commission is nominally paid to the broker by the sponsor or operator (let's say it's eight percent) and the sponsor charges a ten percent management fee which he reports as fully deductible. This could result, if it is disallowed, in your having to refile your tax return, pay the additional tax due on the nondeductible portion, plus a penalty for late taxes.

☐ Acreage costs—Only in the case of abandonment, is acreage cost currently deductible. Usually the sponsor will own or acquire acreage to be retained and amortized over a period if the well is successful. If the well is dry, the to-be abandoned acreage will be assigned to the investors as a currently deductible item.

☐ Intangible drilling cost deductions—Under the provisions of Section 263(c), these are fully deductible as business expense against other income. Where there may be a technical problem is in the revenue sharing arrangement of the partnership. This is getting into the area of program structure which will be covered in detail in the next chapter, but we need to look at the one example now: in all cases the sponsor is motivated by profit. It can be a cash profit, like a management fee. There is almost always some "promotion" in an oil venture. That is, the sponsor usually expects to receive a greater percentage of the revenues of a successful program than he put up in cash. The "standard" deal in the oil business is that the investor will put up to 100 percent of cost to casing point, and 75 percent after casing point for a 75 percent interest in revenues after the investor first gets his money back. This is called "a third for a quarter"—the investor puts up a third of the total for a fourth of the revenues. If a certain filing procedure (with the IRS) is not followed by the sponsor and operator, the right of the investors to deduct 100 percent of the I.D.C. has been questioned on the basis that the ultimate revenue interest, 75 percent which is a kind of equity, is all the investors are entitled to. Proper filings by the operator and sponsor specifying disproportionate allocation of intangibles can, by and large, avoid this.

☐ When These Deductions Should Be Taken—Another problem may be created by the abuse of prepaid drilling contracts. In the case of a well which is started late in the year and continues the intangible drilling expenditure on into the following calendar year, the IRS normally will permit deduction of full intangible drilling cost if the drilling contract is prepaid. Some promoters have taken a rather broad interpretation of this and prey upon the year end tax procrastinators. They sign turnkey drilling contracts late in the year, package them into a limited partnership and then offer them in late December, claiming the investor will receive a full deduction for IDC. If the IRS can prove that this was the intent, the deduction may well be disallowed, at best. If tax fraud can be proven, the consequences can be more serious. Most late year end oil offerings are of questionable quality and often involve overpayment for acreage and drilling costs. The only exceptions would be very shallow wells capable of completion within the calendar year.

☐ Tangible or capital completion costs—These must be amortized over a period of time, and do not constitute a current deduction.

The key to maximizing tax deductions is for the general partner to either borrow the money on behalf of the partnership to pay to non-currently deductible portions of costs, or have someone else pay them. There is a price for doing this, either in terms of repaying borrowed money and the interest charges or giving a percentage of revenues to the party who pays the non-deductible costs.

To summarize, the sales commission, registration and offering expense and tangible (capital) costs of completion either should be borrowed or paid by other than the tax-oriented investors.

If these costs are borrowed, they must be paid back out of production revenues. It is important that the entire revenues not be encumbered so that some cash will be available to distribute to investors to pay taxes on the revenues. This is the "phantom income" bugaboo to be explained later. No more than half the revenues should be encumbered in order to allow for some cash distribution. Otherwise, the investors may end up paying taxes on income never received.

If the money for capital completion costs is paid by someone else, either the sponsor or a third party, he will usually receive some sort of promotion in terms of revenue. That is, he will receive a greater percentage of total revenues than his participation in total costs. As an example, in one SEC registered program which seeks to maximize tax benefits to investors, the sponsor advances the sales commissions and registration and offering expense, to be repaid from one-half the revenues of a successful program. The sponsor also pays all the capital costs of completing the wells—no less than 15 percent of the total program cost—and takes a 40 percent interest in revenues and expenses of production. Bear in mind that in dry holes, there is no completion cost—they constitute a deduction for the investors. Also bear in mind that in an unsuccessful program, that the sponsor may not get his money back that he either advanced or borrowed. This is the reason that he takes a 25 percent promotion—to compensate for not getting the cushion of current deductions and to compensate for the risk of not getting his money back. The investor is cushioned by high current tax deductions.

About 20 percent of the SEC registered programs offered in 1979 were structured to maximize investors' tax deductions at the expense of longer term economics. But this is not the ultimate in tax avoidance vehicles in oil and gas drilling. For those whose primary interest is avoidance of taxes this year and the taking of substantial risks to achieve this, there is a way to deduct more than you invest this year.

SOME EXTRA POINTS—HOW TO DEDUCT MORE THAN YOU INVEST THIS YEAR

This is not generally recommended, but is such an intriguing technique that you should be aware of it. It should be used only by investors in the maximum tax brackets—70 percent—with an operator who has successfully done this a number of times and under the guidance of a tax attorney and accountant who have successfully overseen such tax-oriented ventures before.

The Tax Reform Act of 1976 imposed an "at risk" limitation on deductions taken for oil and gas activities. This means you cannot deduct more money than you personally have at risk. One way of putting your money at risk without writing a check is to sign a personal note.

Another way is to arrange for a letter of credit from your bank. A letter of credit is a promise by your bank to pay a certain amount on your behalf on a specified date, usually to another bank. Your bank will not issue a letter of credit unless you are so substantial that it can do this on your statement alone, which is rare. Since this technique is viable only for very large, very high bracket investors, a letter of credit arrangement for them is possible, although Federal Reserve bank examiners are increasingly critical of the open-ended liability (on the bank's part) of letters of credit.

The scenario will work like this. An operator who has some development prospects to drill, packages an offering in which all deductible expenses are assigned to the investors, providing a theoretical 100 percent deduction. There would need to be several development properties involved, since banks prefer to see a diversification of collateral in a loan (which will be explained shortly).

The capital costs of completing the wells would be borne by someone else, possibly the operator or an oil or gas user, like a refinery or utility. The investors put up their deductible costs, one-half in cash and the other half in the form of letters of credit. The operator uses the letters of credit for a loan at the bank to drill the prospects to the casing point, after which time he or someone else pays for completion of the wells. The wells, if successful, are produced for at least six months, to give an acceptable history of production flow and pressure for an independent engineering study.

Based on an acceptable engineering study, a production payment loan is made to pay off the loan collateralized by the letters of credit. That is, the loan becomes one which is secured by the reserves proved up by the drilling and is amortized by the cash flow from the wells. With the reserves as collateral, the letters of credit may be released. If such a deal is successful, the investor has realized deductions of about double his cash invested, even though he is "at risk" on the full amount. If the reserves and cash flow are not sufficient to support a loan, the letters of credit would be called by the bank and the deduction would end up being within the "at risk" limitation of 100 percent.

Possible Pitfalls When Doing This

Probably such arrangements invite an IRS audit of the partnership, and may involve the individual investors as well. In addition, there are many pitfalls which can appear along the way.

Following is a simple diagram showing the sequence of events which are scheduled to take place to produce this multiple write-off.

Point A is the time at which the partnership closes and investors present their checks and letters of credit. Drilling begins shortly after this. Point B, about three months later, the wells are completed and put on production at Point C. Production continues for six months until Point D. Engineering study and bank evaluation take a month or two, until Point E. At this time, the bank makes the production payment loan and the letters of credit are returned to the investors.

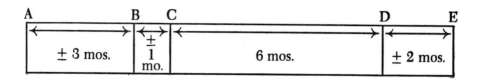

The above diagram assumes that all works like clockwork and the time schedule can be adhered to. Needless to say, all arrangements have to be made with the bank well in advance, with the main question marks being successful well completion and an acceptable engineering study.

Any delay in completing the wells or putting them on production could throw the timetable out of kilter. A two year letter of credit arrangement would give a better cushion if it could be worked out.

The biggest fly in this proposed ointment is that the reserves would not support a large enough production payment loan to fully release the letters of credit. A delay in completing the wells or getting the oil or gas to market would work against this scheme. (If they are proposed gas wells, feeder lines should be adjacent to the drillsites.)

Another potential problem even if the wells are successful is that if the cash flow from the wells goes entirely to liquidate the loan, then this would create "phantom," that is taxable, income without any corresponding cash distribution. Then the investor would have to go into pocket to pay taxes on income never received.

For the 70 percent taxpayer and the somewhat innovative operator with good banking connections, this can work but is not recommended for the great majority of investors.

YOUR PERSONAL INCOME TAX SITUATION

The Federal income tax on earned or personal service income is currently limited to 50 percent of adjusted gross income. According to the tables attached to the instruction booklet on the Form 1040, this occurs at and above the $32,000 level for a taxpayer filing single, and at and above $44,000 for a married couple filing jointly. The effect of inflation has been to throw a large number of people who never expected to be there into the so-called "50 percent bracket"—or maybe they think so. There is not a tax on gross income. The adjusted gross income is taxable after exemptions and deductions.

It is very important that investment in oil be a carefully planned part of your ongoing investment plans. As mentioned earlier, it should give you some spread in time as well as exposure to a good number of wells over this period of time.

Tax planning is an important part of investment planning and should be blueprinted in advance, working with your tax attorney or CPA. You do not get the planned-for benefit of the tax deductions created by a tax incentive investment if you are not taking the deductions against income which is taxed at least fifty percent. For instance, if you are a single taxpayer and your taxable (adjusted gross) income is $38,000. It is true that the top $6,000 is taxed at 50 percent. If you create deductions in excess of $6,000, you are sheltering below the 50 percent bracket, where the benefits begin to diminish.

As a second example, if you are part of a couple filing jointly whose taxable income was $50,000 last year and you anticipated that it would be about the same this year. If you bought a new house early this year on which the taxes and mortgage interest payments totalled $6,000, then you would not want to shelter any more by a tax incentive commitment, because, there again, you are getting into dollars that are taxed at less than fifty percent.

Many oil and gas investments include a possible assessment, even though in the case of most SEC registered programs, they are limited to a range of 25 percent to 100 percent of the original investment. The nature of this assessment may require that you do some cash flow planning along with your tax planning in session with your tax attorney and/or CPA. If the possible assessment for the program you purchased this year for $10,000 is limited to 50 percent for well completions, then that is another $5,000 you may have to write a check for which you will receive very little tax deduction. If, on the other hand, the assessment is for drilling additional development wells created by a discovery, then you will receive a greater deduction because of the intangible drilling cost deduction.

By now you should begin to have a good grasp of the basics of tax benefits available to oil and gas investors and to what length you may go in seeking legal tax avoidance. The degree to which you are willing to sacrifice longer term economic potential for current tax benefits is an important factor in your choice of type of oil and gas investments. Of equal importance, if not greater, is the structure of the program—how costs and revenues are shared. There are seven basic means of sharing revenues in the oil business with a total possibility exceeding five million variations! The following chapter will not attempt to review all these possibilities, but will explain the various types and point out a relatively simple method of comparing what may seem to be apples and oranges to someone who has not been exposed to the oil business before.

4

Run, Pass or Punt?

Now that you have some understanding of the basics of the oil business, and a firm idea of how investment in oil and gas may fit into a long-term investment plan for you and are convinced that you will be in a position to benefit from the tax advantages, what steps you can take to determine what kind of oil and gas venture you want to commit your funds to?

HOW SHOULD YOU APPROACH OIL AND GAS INVESTMENTS?

There are only two reasons to take money which has been going in one direction and point it in another. They are valid if they:

1. ultimately increase your net worth or
2. increase your spendable income.

If investment in oil and gas ventures cannot do one of these for you over the long term, it is not recommended.

The initial consideration for determinining what kind of oil and gas venture to invest in is how to make a choice in a field that is confusingly large. This chapter will first give you some general suggestions for narrowing your choice and then very specifically show you the variety available through the example of a reduced number of offerings.

You will then be told all the varieties of structure which are possible in oil ventures. Structures have been often used as a smokescreen for an undesirable deal. After the possibly confusing variety of structure, you will be shown a relatively simple method of making touchdowns out of home runs, or vice-versa, so that you have a valid means of comparing similar programs.

What Is Not Available In The Lineup

One short comment on what is *not* available—a low-risk program with 100 percent deductibility which has reasonable assurance of an inordinately high return. Do not expect miracles in the oil business unless you can find an officially sanctified sponsor!

A documented example of such a deal was the notorious Home Stake Production scandal. Home Stake was an SEC registered program sold primarily by in-house salesmen from 1964 to 1973. It promised a high tax deduction and projected (not in the prospectus, but in an illegal piece of sales literature, called their "Black Book"), a 350 percent *plus* return. The Home Stake offerings took in over $100 million from investors by promising this super return, even though the prospectus showed very clearly that no program had ever even gotten its investors' money back. The illusion of high return was nurtured by taking some of the money of new investors and paying it out to the older investors to make it appear that such a return might be possible. An excellent and well-documented book on the Home Stake scandal was published in 1977, entitled *Stealing from the Rich*. Read it before you take a chance on getting rich quick by investing in oil.

What Is Available In The Lineup

In looking at what is available in registered programs, here are four viewpoints, all important in making your choice:

1. Tax orientation;
2. Risk orientation;
3. Percent of dollars invested "into the ground" (money available to the program after front end changes); and
4. Structure possibilities.

All of these possibilities are discussed in detail throughout this chapter. Towards the end of the chapter a relatively simple means of comparing similar programs will be shown, and examples given.

The Lineup In General Terms

Tax Orientation: This is very narrow in SEC'd programs. The normal range of first year deductions will vary from 50 percent to 95 percent or a bit more. There are some hybrids which have almost no up front tax benefits, and we'll deal with them shortly.

Risk Orientation: The risk dealt with here is the risk assumed by investment in a particular segment of the oil business. Here is where we can begin to pare the list of possible investments based on a lack of past history. We will consider only those programs which have been offered for ten years or more. These have documentation of a ten year record.

This does not mean that those programs without such a history may not be as good, or even better deals than the older ones. It simply gives us a solid basis on which to decide, based on past history, what kind of investment performance can be documented.

For comparison purposes, cutting out the "newer" programs gives us few enough offerings to make some comparisons that are meaningful because they show trends without overpowering the reader with too many statistics.

The number of SEC registered drilling programs has just about doubled in the past two years, and some of the newer programs have a fairer structure than some of the older ones. This trend will continue to give the investor a better shake as time and competition proceed.

In 1979, there were programs offered by 75 different sponsors. Of these, *29 were primarily exploratory* (60 percent or more of the money went into exploration), *six were for development drilling* (on proven and semi-proven acreage), *32 were called "balanced" programs* (no more than 50 percent exploration, averaging about 30 percent; the balance going into lower risk proven and semi-proven drilling), and *nine were hybrids* which generally don't drill at all, and consequently offer no front end tax benefits of note. These hybrids either *buy producing properties, buy royalty interests*, or supply the capital cost of completing wells already drilled to the casing point.

In order to further narrow our list of potential oil investments, let us remove from consideration the nine hybrids which offer only minimal tax benefits. The next smaller category are the development only (85 percent or more) operators.

Of these six, only one has a ten-year history. The only significant payout in this group was achieved in a 1971 program which had a double stroke of good timing. First, a shallower production formation than the target structure was encountered, which allowed some dual completions (getting production from two formations) which was compounded by the four-fold OPEC price increase in 1973. The other sponsors of these low risk programs have not enough history to bear out the economics of development-only drilling, although the probabilities of satisfactory performance for investors seem high. The hybrids and the development-only programs will be removed from consideration for investment.

Numerically, the greatest number of registered programs offered are "balanced" programs, offering participation in a balance of exploratory (not over 50 percent, averaging about 30 percent) and development drilling. These 32 programs have been able to achieve some cash distribution more quickly than the exploratory-only programs because the development wells can be put into production more quickly. However, only five of these balanced programs have a ten-year history, and it is these five that we will consider in this category.

Of the 29 exploratory programs offered, only nine have a ten-year history. These programs, which offer high risk exposure to the possibility of higher than average returns, will get our scrutiny.

For consideration, we are left with nine exploration and five balanced programs with ten-year histories for initial consideration. In general, based on available statistics, what are the characteristics of the exploration and the balanced programs?

Characteristics of Exploration Programs:

- Sporadic results;
- Lower success ratio than balanced programs;
- Initial distributions of cash come much later than the balanced programs;
- Returns range from zero to over 300 percent.

Characteristics of Balanced Programs:

- Far higher success ratios than exploratory programs;
- Earlier distributions of cash from development wells;
- Higher ratio of programs which achieve payout;
- Lower overall return to investors in paid out programs than sucessful exploratory programs.

A Comparison Of Performance In Successful Programs

Successful programs are those which have achieved payout, or have gotten all the investors' money back. The importance of payout's definition will be touched on in the discussion of structure possibilities later in this chapter.

The nine exploratory sponsors have achieved payout in 13 programs in the past ten years through 1978. The average return to the investors in these successful programs has been 245 percent. Most of these programs still are producing, so the return will increase until the properties are fully produced.

The five sponsors of balanced programs have achieved payout in ten programs in the ten-year period. The average return to the investors through 1978 has been 154 percent in the successful programs.

On the negative side, the balanced programs with the ten-year histories show only two programs over three-years old, which have made no cash distributions.

The nine exploratory programs have almost as many programs which have made no cash distributions as they have had successful programs—a total of 12 which have been operating for four years or more have made no cash distribution. In defense of the exploration programs, some of these have utilized borrowed money for additional development and their revenues are pledged to repaying these loans before any cash distributions. Also, some of the very successful exploration programs have chosen to plow back production revenues into further development, rather than distributing them to investors. The nature of exploration is that the greater amount of development, the greater need for funds.

In line with the contention that there are only two reasons for making a change in investments—increasing net worth or spendable income—is the fact of dramatically increasing oil and gas prices. The exploration program which creates the greatest number of barrels or cubic feet *in the ground* in a time of constantly higher oil and gas prices is the one which serves best the investor with long term goals in mind. It is difficult to explain to a non-oil investor that the ideal situation in exploration would be to make a discovery so large that no cash might be distributed for over ten years, the revenues being plowed backed into additional development drilling, and hence, into reserves in the ground.

Track Record And The
Sponsor's Past Performance

Chapter 6 will discuss track record in greater detail; however, at this point you should generally be aware of what its potential impact could be on a program.

To make an oil investment on the basis of structure alone is a mistake. Although the track record is important for determining how many dollars were distributed in cash, it is often more important to know what the sponsor has accomplished in light of his goals.

That is to say, if you invest in a program which is mainly exploratory (say 85 percent or more) and the program has a fairly consistent record of early cash distributions, then it would appear that the sponsor is drilling prospects which are closer in to known production than those of greater risk which might produce a discovery not only worthy of additional development drilling, but also capable of producing reserves which are significant in relation to the money at risk. Even in a large diversified exploratory program, the numerical majority of the programs probably will not return the original investment. This is why it is necessary for them to drill those prospects which have the potential to make the good programs outstanding in terms of return.

On the other hand, if the program is predominantly development drilling, it should show early cash distribution with fair consistency. A really big return may occur on rare occasions in a development program, but this is not the type of return which should happen. If a development program had several offerings which provided the kind of return that shows up in exploratory drilling (none have, so far) it would indicate that the program was likely drilling higher risk prospects than should be in this type of program.

Track record should not be geared to absolute numbers, but to judging how well the sponsor has served the needs of his investors. One very misleading statistic which is used in the "success ratio." The success ratio means the percentage of wells drilled which have been completed as producers. That is, if ten wells are drilled, and five are completed, then that is a 50 percent success ratio. BUT, if the wells do not get all the investors' money back, then the success ratio is meaningless.

Cash payout can be misleading on the downside in an exploratory program. As stated earlier, the ideal exploratory program is one in which a discovery is made which is so large that it requires another ten years of development drilling to prove up all the reserves discovered. During this time, no cash would be distributed because of the pressure of funds needed for development drilling. Some of the largest and most successful programs have made only token cash distributions. A program of this type which has a cash redemption feature can be judged on the basis of this cash out, giving weight to the heavy discount because of the fact that this is a measure of value of a resource underground. Those exploratory programs which did not distribute cash obtained by selling oil at $12 per barrel in 1978 because of the need to do more development drilling, will likely have well-satisfied investors when the additional reserves brought to market because of the development drilling are marketed at $30 per barrel, or better.

To summarize, the opportunity to get no return in exploration is much greater than in a balanced program. The opportunity for substantial gain in a balanced program is much less than in exploration. Over the long term, you will draw fewer blanks in a balanced program, but there will not be as many big returns.

Historically, over the ten-year period under study, if you had invested in exploration, you would have some programs which return nothing, and some which show big gains. In making investments in balanced programs, you dramatically lessen the chances of no return, but also diminish the probability of large returns. You and your tax and investment advisers will have to determine which best suits your long-term investment plans.

HOW TO ASSESS THE POTENTIAL OF OIL AND GAS PROGRAMS BASED ON STRUCTURE

"Structure" in oil programs is the formula for determining cost and revenue sharing between the investors and the sponsors. We have touched on costs in terms of fees, front-end and ongoing, and will bring them back in shortly in order to compare similar programs. For the purposes of this section, let us consider only cost and revenue-sharing plans.

Structure is the most deceptive part of oil investments for most investors. It has been used as a smokescreen for some very poor offerings. The important thing in oil and gas investments is the ability of the sponsor or operator to make economic successes of his programs by finding enough oil or gas to get the investors their money back and provide a competitive return.

The worst structured program, if enough oil or gas is found, can show superior returns to the investors. The best structure around cannot make up for finding insufficient oil or gas to at least pay out the investors. A seemingly favorable structure may be an attempt to hide other profits for the sponsor which are not immediately apparent. These comments do not apply to many SEC registered programs, but will, sadly, find application in analyzing those Rule 146 offerings which are not foursquare. The purpose of reviewing structure here is to allow a meaningful comparison of SEC registered programs in terms of how structure may affect the investor in like programs which have had equivalent success in finding oil.

Here are the seven basic formulae for investor/sponsor sharing of costs and revenues with comments on how they may affect the investor:

1. Overrides: An override is properly called an overriding royalty interest, and is a percentage of gross revenues before operating expenses. A positive use of overrides is for additional compensation of technical personnel of the sponsor. That is, the program may have a small override on discoveries made, to provide additional compensation to the geologists who did the work which resulted in the discovery. This is a form of profit-sharing for technical personnel, and is a means of tying capable people to the sponsor's organization.

Objectionable overrides are those which accrue to the sponsor directly. The reason that they are objectionable is that no expense or risk is borne by the operator. He has, with an override, an economic incentive to complete wells which may not pay out the investor. He gets his override from the first barrel, and has no risk at all.

2. Net Profit Interest: A net profit interest is a percentage interest in production after operating expenses. It is less burdensome than an override in that if the well is not profitable, there will be no net profits. Most net profit interests are activated on payout—the investors' recoupment of his original commitment. This is not commonly used at present.

3. Carried Interest: A carried interest is one in which the sponsor may bear none of the expense of drilling the well to the casing point, but may share completion costs and production revenues up to a certain percent. A 25 percent carried interest would be one in which the investors put up all the money for drilling. After the casing point and the decision to complete the well has been made, the sponsor shares in 25 percent of the cost of completing the well and takes 25 percent of the revenue after operating expenses. The investor puts up 100 percent of the risk money (and receives all the tax deduction of the intangible drilling cost) and 75 percent of the after expense revenue. A 25 percent carried interest is often called "a third for a quarter" and is alluded to as a "standard industry deal." The investor puts 100 percent of the risk money and gets a 75 percent interest in production. He puts up one-third of the cost of drilling for each one-quarter of production; hence, a "third for a quarter."

4. Reversionary Working Interest: This is working interest which "reverts" to the sponsor after a certain point, usually payout to the investors. A sponsor who puts up 25 percent of the drilling money might structure his programs to provide that he would also take 25 percent of production until the investors get their money back. At that point, he would receive a reversionary working interest of an additional 25 percent, bringing the division of production to a 50–50 split. The definition of payout can make a dramatic difference as to when the reversionary working interest is triggered. If the definition of payout is on a "prospect-by-prospect" basis, this means that dry holes only count for tax deductions and payout occurs when the investors have been made whole on *successful wells only.* Probably a fairer definition is "total program payout." That is, payout occurs when the investors have received back all their money from all wells, both dry and successful.

5. Functional Allocation: In functional allocation, the investors bear the currently deductible expenses and the sponsor bears the capital costs. Revenues are shared in proportion to the total cost of the well. For example, if the deductible portion of the well's cost is 70 percent of the total, and the capital cost is 30 percent, then revenues would be shared 70–30. Under this formula, the investors bear all costs of dry holes and abandoned acreage and of course, get current tax deductions for these expenses. Since these expenses can vary considerably from well to well, it is a difficult problem accounting wise. The variation that follows is more popular.

6. Functional Allocation of Costs and Arbitrary Allocation of Revenues: Costs are allocated in the same way, deductible costs to investors and capital costs to the sponsors. Revenues are then shared on an arbitrary percentage. The most favorable in SEC'd programs in the past ten years has been one program which offered an 80–20 revenue split with investors who had invested in an earlier program promising a 70–30 split, an average of 75–25. The current offerings take as much as 40 percent of revenues for the sponsor who puts up capital costs.

7. Other: These do not apply to the SEC registered programs with a ten-year history, but have shown up recently in some newer ones. These are generally profits which are not hidden but are stated in dollars rather than promising that conflicts of interest will be avoided by using competitive pricing. "Other" ways of making profit mean generally, an opportunity for the sponsor to take a locked-in additional profit at the expense of his captive investor group. These include:

a. Turnkey drilling contracts: at non-competitive prices. A program sponsor who owns drilling rigs would naturally be inclined to operate his own rigs rather than those of someone else. If he agrees in writing in the offering document and in the partnership papers to drill the wells at prices that are competitive in the area of interest, then this removes much of the conflict of interest. If the sponsor simply agrees to drill the wells at a dollar price, then it is incumbent upon the investor to verify that the cost really *is* competitive.

b. Overrides retained by the sponsor: The conflict of interest here has been commented on at page 99.

c. Selling leases at a profit to the partnership: If the sponsor owns leases, they should be passed on at cost to the investors unless it is clearly stated that a part of the sponsors' compensation is profiting from the sale of the leases. A thinly veiled means of profiting from sponsor lease ownership is for the sponsor to contribute leases of uncertain or unstated value in return for a percentage of the program. Most sponsors retain ownership of the leases until the acreage is to be abandoned, at which time it is assigned at cost to the investors, who receive a deduction for abandoned acreage.

d. Selling supplies or services to the investors at non-competitive prices: If an affiliate of the sponsor is a vendor of supplies, like drillpipe, mud and the like, there is the possibility of a conflict of interest. If this potential conflict of interest is clearly spelled out and the sponsor is committed to selling to the partnership at "prices which are generally competitive," then this lessens the potential conflict. Where there is solely an admission that the sponsor is affiliated with a supply company with no promise of competitive pricing, this situation should be avoided.

e. Making a profit on personnel: is a practice that seldom occurs these days. It has worked in the past like this: The sponsor has other activities than the partnership which he is offering and has personnel not specifically employed in partnership activities—usually technical people. If the sponsor retains the right to bill out the services of a technical person at, say $30 per hour, when the going rate for such people in the area is $20, then he is profiting from his personnel's services. This conflict can be avoided by the sponsor agreeing to pro rate at actual cost the time spent by his personnel on a particular program.

There are other opportunities for sponsor profit which are not apparent to those who do not know the oil business. In fact, some brokerage firms have (in jest, I am sure) been offered drilling packages which charged no management fee and had no overrides or promotion. Of course, they would charge a high price for drilling the wells with their own rigs, sell supplies at a non-competitive markup and profit from the services of personnel. You will never see all these profit sources show up at once, nowadays, and seldom in an SEC registered program.

Where the "other" profits slip in is generally in Rule 146 exemptions where they rate only one or two lines in the offering document, but may produce a large amount of undisclosed profit. Chapter 5 will deal with dissecting a Rule 146 (or an SEC registration, if you wish) with detailed questions.

For now, however, the above section on structure may well have served to confuse you temporarily. You need to know all the terms which may make up a potential smoke screen before you can go about clearing the smoke screen.

How Can You Clear The Smoke Screen

With seven basic profit schemes (including all the "other" as one), there are a total of 5,764,801 possible ways of structuring an oil deal. Clearing the smoke screen will be a matter of translating this unmanageable number of possibilities into a *lingua franca* which we all understand.

What you can do in comparing like structured programs is to assume like success in finding oil or gas and then translate this into the investors' percentage interest in this production. You have then a guideline which turns the whole fruit basket into the same apples. Once again, this does not show how much money you can make as an investor, but given like success in finding hydrocarbons, you can see quickly which is the more potentially profitable offering.

Net Revenue Interest to the Investors

When acreage to be drilled is leased, there is always a landowners' royalty, or lease burden. If there is an additional overriding royalty interest, then this, too, is a lease burden. The interest in production from a given lease after lease burden, is the *working interest in the prospect.*

The way the revenue is shared between sponsor and the investors (both before and after payout, if there is a difference) is the partnership working interest. Oil investors find this most confusing because the term *working interest* is used in both cases. Here's an example.

If a lease has a 12½ percent landowners' royalty, then the working interest in the prospect is 87½ percent. That is, if 100 percent interest in the prospect is bought by a partnership, then their interest in the prospect is 100 percent. But their interest in production is 100 percent of 87½ percent. Now, if the revenue sharing arrangement in the partnership is 75 percent to the investors and 25 percent to the sponsor, then the net revenue interest to the investors in this prospect, if successful, is .75 × .875, or .65625. In other words, if the investors put up all the money to drill the prospect and the sponsor takes a 25 percent promoted interest, the investors receive about 66 percent of the revenues and pay about 66 percent of the operating expenses.

Now, if there is an *additional reversionary* working interest to be taken after payout, then the net revenue interest of the investors changes again. For example, if the revenues after payout change to 50–50, then the investors' net revenue interest after payout is .50 × .875, or .4375, about 44 percent.

Things Which Affect Net Revenue Interest

Where there is a change of revenue upon payout, how payout is defined becomes very important to the investor. More and more, payout is being defined by sponsors as total return of all monies invested, including the front end charges. This is called "total program payout"—getting 100 percent of the dollars invested back to the investors before the promotion to the sponsor increases.

Mentioned earlier was payout on a prospect-by-prospect basis. That is, dry holes (usually including the cost of abandoned acreage) are counted only as tax deductions. Only the cost of successful wells is included in the computation of payout. In a hypothetical exploratory program which is a $1,000,000 venture which proposes to take equal interests in ten exploratory wells, if eight of the exploration wells are dry, then those count only as tax deductions for the investors. Payout occurs, on a prospect-by-prospect basis here, when the investors have gotten back only the cost of successful wells. If the interest in the ten wells were equal, then payout, as defined, would occur when the investors, who had put up the $1,000,000, had gotten back $200,000. (They did get $800,000 in current tax deductions.)

Another variation on the theme of varying payout definition is in connection with programs featuring functional allocation on both costs and revenues, in which the investors pay the deductible costs and sponsor pays the capital completion costs. Revenues are shared according to the allocation of costs in relation to the total. In one functional allocation program, there was no promotion before payout. That is, the investors were credited with 100% of *gross revenues* from production on a prospect-by-prospect basis until the *gross revenues* equalled the cost of the successful wells. All dry hole costs were assigned to the investors as tax deductions. Since this was an exploratory program, and additional development drilling around the successful exploratory wells was required, there was, in fact, no distribution of cash to the investors because this money was needed for development wells. The investors were "paid out" by crediting gross revenues to their capital accounts, which were later debited for additional development drilling costs. The program provided that the revenues would be divided 75–25 after payout, as defined. No actual cash was distributed from this program until all development drilling was completed.

This does not condemn functional allocation, but appears to have been used primarily as a marketing tool to state that "all initial production revenues will accrue to the capital accounts of the limited partners." Upon payout of successful wells, the General Partner will receive 25 percent of revenues and the limited partners 75 percent. An additional tax benefit did accrue to the investors in the form of additional tax deductions from the intangible drilling costs of development wells. Pure functional allocation is discouraged by most oil accounting firms as being difficult in terms of allocating costs. Far more common is functional allocation of cost, and an arbitrary sharing of revenues.

The purpose of this dissection of structure is to make the investor ask the question, "100 percent of WHAT?, or "75 percent of WHAT?"

Another consideration is the type of prospects to be drilled and this can only be dealt with in very general terms. Most new oil and gas wells go through three stages of production: the initial or *flush* stage, in which the pressure and rate of flow are several times what they will settle down to in the second phase, *stable production*. During the period of stable production, there is some decline, which is relatively predictable in rate of decline for some time. The final phase, or *decline* phase, shows marked dropoff in production at a fairly rapid rate to depletion. Some wells, particularly shallow gas wells in many areas, have a relatively short but very flush period, and go directly into a rapid decline and deplete within a very few years. In this latter type of production, the sponsor can profit well from rather light promotion both before and after payout, because the initial profit from promotion comes up front. Where the nature of prospects to be drilled is that of fairly long life of the stable production phase, the promotion needs to be greater on the back end to take advantage of production that continues for a long period.

The pricing of acreage will be largely determined by the nature of the venture. The most important part of pricing proven and semi-proven (development) acreage, from the landowners' point of view, is the royalty he negotiates. Whereas in wildcat acreage, overrides to landowers of 12½ percent (an eighth) are still common in many prospective areas, overrides on close-in, proven acreage are sometimes 20 percent. This is a premium of 62.5 percent over the eighth royalty and dramatically affects the net revenue interest to the investor. This is one of the reasons that development drilling is normally not as potentially profitable as exploration. On the other hand, it is nowhere close to so risky. Now go back and read the first four paragraphs of this section until you can calculate *net revenue interest*.

HOW TO AVOID BEING SANDBAGGED, RED-DOGGED, DOUBLE-TEAMED, BLIND-SIDED AND CONCUSSED

If you are new to oil investment and particularly, if you are an investor who has become somewhat embittered because of a "can't win" oil investment you got talked into before you were very knowledgeable, you should limit your choice of investments to those programs which are registered with the SEC and cleared for offering in the state in which you are domiciled.

If you go into any oil investment without knowing (or knowing that a responsible and knowledgeable party has checked out) most of the ascertainable facts about the deal, then that is analogous to going into a football game without your helmet on and with blinders to boot! Without thorough investigation of both the people and the deal, you are without the helmet of full disclosure and are further hampered by the blinders of incomplete knowledge and unpracticed judgment.

The primary reason for this strong recommendation of the fully registered program is not so much because of the disclosure requirements of the regulatory bodies, although this is very important. The primary reason is the protection of the due diligence studies by the brokerage firms who underwrite these programs. The regulatory bodies are charged only with seeing that "full and fair disclosure" is made to all prospective investors. They have no interest, officially, as to whether a program may or may not be a good investment. (Some state regulators do impose this business judgment.) For instance, one registered real estate offering in 1972 clearly stated on the second page of the prospectus, that if all the fees and charges permitted in accordance with the prospectus and partnership papers were taken, this would total 84 percent of the capital supplied by investors. To the credit of the investing public, this offering was withdrawn.

To overstate the case, if a prospectus stated very clearly that the proceeds of the offering were to go into the sponsor's pocket and he planned to leave for Brazil shortly thereafter, the regulatory authorities could conceivably say that this constituted full and fair disclosure.

The due diligence procedure of major brokerage houses is an important protection for the potential investor in oil and gas. This concerns itself not only with the reliability of the information presented, but also, with how reasonable a chance the program has, over the long term, to produce tangible results for the qualified oil and gas investor. This is based on a tremendous amount of digging into other information not generally available to the public.

The Steps That Go Into Due Diligence Studies Of Major Brokerage Firms

Nearly all SEC registered programs today are sold through brokerage firms, who serve as best efforts underwriters. They have a liability as underwriters, and an ongoing interest in offering to their investors deals which can produce good economic results. A drilling program does not usually end up on a list of offerings of an underwriter merely by happenstance, but as the result of long and careful study by the brokerage firm. Below are some of the procedures followed in a full due diligence study, with comments on their importance as investor protections.

First-Hand Knowledge Of Sponsors' Personnel: Most brokerage firms assume the role of underwriter only after they have known the sponsors' firms for some time. A part of the due diligence study is finding complete information on the backgrounds of management personnel. As well, the study will give an opportunity for brokerage personnel to get to know the oil company's people personally. This personal contact allows the brokerage firms to know exactly who in the operating company is responsible for the performance of what duties. In addition to determining that the people are of the caliber the underwriter wants running his clients' investments, it is an aid in the continual updating of information which most underwriters rely upon.

How Brokers Utilize Independent Experts: By now you realize just how complex the oil business has become. The underwriters realize this, too, and to fill in the gaps in their technical knowledge, they will commonly retain experts in the field to pass judgment on investment decisions and information which the sponsor is responsible for. Almost all the SEC registered programs are blind pools; that is, they invest the money in unspecified properties. This gives a theoretical carte blanche to the sponsor to drill just about however and whatever he pleases, within the limitations of the terms of the partnership agreement.

The Independent Geologist: For this reason, the underwriter will often call in an independent geologist to review the prospects which a program proposes to drill. However, a sponsor may give details of certain prospects to an underwriter which are not supplied to the potential investor. These may be actual prospects to be drilled, or "typical" prospects in the area of interest.

It is this information that can be given to an independent geologist. This geologist will be experienced in the area of interest, and is paid only to pass judgment on the merit of the types of prospects chosen by the sponsor. This is particularly important to a relatively new SEC'd program which has not yet established a track record old enough to be considered proof of the ability to produce consistently.

The Independent Engineer: In programs which have been around for a few years, it is important to have independent engineers estimate recoverable reserves and future net revenue, based on an independent study. Although independent engineers are not necessarily smarter than in-house engineers, they can be more objective. While you can't spend the proceeds of an independent engineering study, it is important that the conflict of interest inherent in an in-house study be removed. An estimate which is either too high or too low may mislead the investor. If the estimate is too high and its purpose is to bring the investor back into future programs, then this is misleading. If the purpose of the study is to allow the sponsor to repurchase the investor's interest and the estimate is too low, then this, too, is a disservice. While petroleum engineering is not yet a precise science in estimating reserves, it is the best assurance available. Most oil oriented banks will lend from 50 percent to 75 percent of the discounted future net revenue of oil in the ground, which could be construed as market value at the time of the study. This bank-approved percentage of oil's market value compares favorably with the commonly accepted 70 percent which is a usual benchmark for a residential real estate loan.

The Independent Accountant And Attorney: Very often independent accountants are called in by underwriters to verify that not only are financial records of the sponsor in tip-top shape, *but that the deductions claimed will be supportable if challenged by the tax authorities.*

Finally, the attorneys for the underwriter will ride herd on counsel for the issuer to see that, among many other things, the partnership papers are drawn so that the likelihood of having an invalid limited partnership is minimized.

The expense of all these experts for one small multiple well investment alone *might exceed the average investment* in a SEC registered program. A part of the reason for recommending these programs is that using outside experts in a due diligence study is included as a matter of course.

What It Costs For These Protections

None of these investor protections come for free, of course. Investors pay for the protections provided by underwriting firms by purchasing the programs sponsored by the firms. The seven percent to eight percent commission charged for acquiring the drilling program through an underwriter pays for the initial due diligence study, the retention of experts, *and a continuing interest in these programs.* Do not think that when you purchase a drilling program that the entire commission goes to the broker in the branch who spent time with you explaining the program. He often gets less than half this commission. The rest of it goes to pay for investor protection and for the scrutiny that your personal broker cannot afford the time to make. By giving up a portion of his commission, he, too, is buying protection against the known general pitfalls of any investment, even before giving any weight to the risks of investment in oil.

The Brokerage Firm's Area Knowledge Of The Oil Industry

As mentioned earlier in this chapter, one of the problems which we also solve by considering only the SEC registered programs is that of making a choice in a field that is confusingly large. There are about 10,000 operating oil companies. Hundreds of these companies finance the drilling of wells by offering interests to persons outside the company. This means that there are likely thousands of offerings made to oil investors each year, from single well deals on up through the multi-million dollar bids for offshore acreage. In addition, these investments can be made in almost three dozen oil producing states. They are available in such a profusion that the more you look, the more confused you become, unless you find some way to limit the scope of your choice. Limiting your choice to the SEC'd programs gives an adequate array of product to choose from and cuts the total under consideration to about 75, in 1979.

In addition to the variety of types of offerings, these occur, as mentioned, all over the oil patch. Unless an investor has some expertise of the oil business in an area, the varying nature of drilling in different areas is additionally confusing.

Most brokerage firms which perform the underwriting function have good background knowledge in their research, corporate finance and tax shelter departments. The smaller regional firms, particularly those domiciled in oil productive areas, have possibly even more knowledge of the nature of oil and gas ventures in their locales. The larger firms all have branch offices in many oil productive areas and have familiarity with the area through local personnel as well as experts in headquarters. The point here is that the underwriters have enough background knowledge of the oil industry in general and oil geography in particular, to be able to make valid comparisons. They are in a position to decide whether the structure of a deal is fair compared to a great variety they have looked at before. In addition, they have the ability to judge the deal based on what the particular area of interest has to offer in terms of both opportunities and pitfalls.

This wide-ranging knowledge and access to detailed information in a variety of areas is part of the expertise which is put to work in due diligence studies, and adds to the appeal of sticking with the registered programs.

Most underwriting firms have no interest in selling an oil program on a one-year or one-shot basis. Once they have established a relationship with a drilling program sponsor, they like to stick with them. The reasons for this are the high cost of due diligence studies and the high personnel time cost requirements. Because the interest of an underwriter is ongoing, the firm continues to monitor carefully the sponsors' activities. This usually entails visits several times per year by analysts, corporate finance personnel, and tax shelter people. This ongoing function is important over a period of years for the investor who invests recurrently, to make sure that everything that looked shipshape on the initial due diligence study stays that way.

HOW TO MAKE YOUR INVESTMENT CHOICE

Your first move in planning to make oil and gas investment a part of your ongoing investment program is to arrange a conference with your CPA, tax attorney or tax advisor. You will need to work with him to project an expected five year plan in which you will give heavy emphasis to the expected tax burden you may be facing. Second, you should do a rough cash flow analysis of your recurring expenses and expected future expenses. Finally, you need to think in terms of estate planning and your estate's liquid position. This is particularly important in light of both the short term total illiquidity of oil investments and the marked disadvantages of taking the heavy discount in later years levied on those programs that do have a right of liquidation.

If you are to become involved in tax oriented investments over a period you should make a tax planning session an annual event, so that you can update your needs as they change. A good time to do this is early in the year, for example, when you confer with your tax advisor on last year's tax returns. This gives you adequate time to plan for the coming taxable year.

Your next step, if you agree that you are a recipient who will qualify for the advice given in this chapter is to meet with your broker to see what his firm has to offer in the SEC registered programs. Most firms have some variety of offerings. In outlining your personal tax savings needs, your willingness to assume risk and the amount of funds you expect to have available to invest in oil and gas, will give him valuable information in trying to guide you into the programs his firm sponsors whose aims most closely parallel yours.

Gut Reaction to the Bossman

Most books written on investments warn against making investment decisions based on uninformed emotional reaction. This is by and large good advice. However, utilizing (to the degree you feel you can trust) your emotional reaction to an individual, can assist you in making your final choice of an SEC registered oil program.

Making an uninformed emotional decision is somewhat analogous to expecting that a stallion charging up a hill will veer around you just because you are standing there with roller skates on. Chances are you'll get trampled. However, if you're heading up the hill, maybe you can grab a hold of his tail and get where you're going faster. You may also trip along the way and skin your knee—but you didn't get trampled.

To draw a further analogy, just because you make an investment in an oil program, is not going to change the direction it has been heading. What you want to know is, first, "Am I heading in the same direction?" Second, "Shall I take a chance on a financial skinned knee in order to get where I'm going more quickly?"

By meeting with your tax advisor and knowing yourself, you have determined the direction you are heading. By comparing several types of oil investments, you have gotten an indication (from past performance) which direction they have been heading. If you are both heading for the same compass point, you have an opportunity to make an informed emotional decision, based on how you like what the head man of the program's sponsoring organizations has to say.

Most of the chief executives of most of the oil programs spend a lot of time on the road, making group presentations to potential investors. The chances are overwhelming that more than once during the coming year, the top management of the program or programs you are seriously considering for investment will make such a presentation in your area. Defer your investment decision until you have had a chance to hear his presentation. Take an opportunity to speak with him personally after the presentation. He will be happy to answer your questions.

Now for your gut reaction: did meeting the man who will be ultimately responsible for the investment of your oil dollars add to or detract from your penchant to invest in his program? If your reaction was largely negative, make another choice and go to hear a presentation by another bossman. If this presentation leaves you with a more positive feeling, then you are probably ready to buy. Get out your checkbook and write the first of three to five annual checks which will save you tax dollars and offer you a chance to reach your investment goals more quickly.

"Game" does not always mean a frivolous pastime. It can be a synonym for "strategy." The decision-making strategy outlined above—the distillation of twenty-five years' observation and experience—is reproduced below in graphic form. Call it a game board if you will, but it does represent the steps taken by many successful investors in implementing their investment strategy.

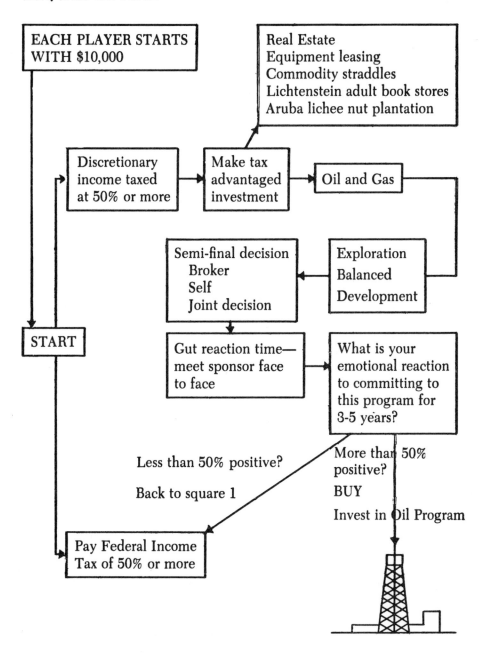

The Energy Investment Game

For those who are anticipating investments of sufficient size to warrant the retention of experts, the following chapter is devoted, since specified prospects are often a feature of Rule 146 exempted offerings. The questions to be answered are largely those which would be asked during the course of a due diligence study by a brokerage firm.

5

Time Out for
Questions from the Referee

Although the majority of readers will agree at this juncture that they are probably best served by sticking with the SEC registered programs, some will want to seriously consider the possibility of making an investment in a Rule 146 offering. Also, those who do go into the SEC'd programs, although they have done so partly because of the due diligence efforts of the brokerage house through which they bought, may want to know more about programs they have bought. This chapter will give you an idea of the scope of a due diligence study. If you are aware of all the questions that need to be answered, prior to getting involved in an investment, you should save some time and money.

WHAT YOU SHOULD CONSIDER PRIOR TO INVESTING
IN A 146 OFFERING?

The primary reasons for investing in a 146 offering are either that the front end load is less than that of a comparable registered program or that it offers specified properties. If neither of these elements is present, then it is hard to justify recommending this exemption from registration. The simple snob appeal of getting into an oil venture just because it is limited to 35 investors is a poor reason for choosing this investment medium.

As stated earlier, few 146 offerings entail less than a $25,000 investment. If they are smaller than this, it is unlikely that they will offer adequate diversification. On the other hand, this is a large enough investment for the potential investor to make a personal call on the sponsor (or pay someone to do this).

If you are considering a 146 offered through a brokerage firm, then it, too, has had due diligence scrutiny and, for the same reason as the registered program, will probably have an equivalent front end load (For a discussion of front end costs, see chapter 2, page 60. In this case, your primary reason for buying will be the attraction of the specified prospects.

The first part of this chapter of inquiry will be in question and comment format. The second part will be checklists of questions. Answers to many of these questions will not be available if the sponsor has not ever made such an offering before. If this is the case, let his first investors be the people who have known him or done business with him for some time. Don't let an issuer experiment on you. Some sponsors feel that a good way to bring in outside investors is to start out by putting a toe in the water with a 146. They may decide after one or two tries that it is not worth the trouble and they will once again concentrate on their former, fewer, private investors. Stick with known sponsors who are committed to financing their ventures by the quasi-private medium of the 146.

There will be five segments to this inquisition: the Preliminaries, the People, the Place, the Program, and the Performance.

PRELIMINARY QUESTIONS TO ANSWER BEFORE CONSIDERING A 146

Question: How many 146 offerings has the sponsor issued?

Comment: Find out the dollar amount and how many programs. If there have been enough to constitute an "integration" problem with the SEC at a later date, then this can work a hardship on future investors. (To get this information consult the sponsor or his attorneys.)

Q: Has the same firm of attorneys been used to draw up past offering documents in 146 offerings?

C: The firm must be experienced in drawing up not only oil oriented offering documents, but also be experienced enough with partnership law and IRS scrutiny to avoid a disallowance of the validity of the partnership or expected deductions.

Q: Will an advance ruling (as to partnership validity) be requested from the IRS?

C: Probably not, because this takes about five to six months and would probably prevent having the prospects specified. This leads to the next question:

Q: How many legal opinions on limited partnerships has the law firm given? (As to partnership validity.)

C: Experience is what you are buying, not thrills. (To get this information write a letter to the law firm who gave opinion or see attorney if local.)

Q: Has the IRS questioned the validity of any past limited partnerships?

C: In 1977, the IRS stated that it would attempt to audit up to a quarter of all tax-oriented programs each year, which produced an aggregate deduction over $25,000. If they have been successful in this, it means that they are scrutinizing every tax shelter program once every four years.

Q: Have any 146 offerings been withdrawn because of the inability of the sponsor to raise the minimum?

C: A consistent record of getting his programs into the ground will save you the disappointment of thinking you are getting into a deal you have investigated, only to find that there are not enough investors to activate it. (To get this information simply ask the sponsor or his attorney.)

Q: Were you asked to acknowledge receipt of the offering document and did the preliminary qualification questionnaire include a representation as to your net worth and/or income?

C: This was commented on in Chapter 1 where sample questionnaires are also provided.

Q: Is the investor qualification questionnaire which must be filled out before subscribing sufficiently detailed for your comfort?

C: This is particularly important in an offering which is larger than the $25,000 minimum mentioned earlier, especially if it is an assessible program. Just as you want to be certain that the program will get off the ground, you want to be certain that all the investors are substantial as you are and can comfortably meet the assessment when it comes. Probably the sponsor can pick up the slack, but it will be a smoother program if all investors meet overcalls in a timely manner.

Q: Are investor communications from earlier programs available for your perusal?

C: The quality of investor communications during the administration of the program is important.

Q: When will the investor get out final information for tax purposes, based on his past performance?

C: It will probably be later than your tax accountant likes, but in some cases, where the sponsor and operator are the same, it could be consistently sooner than some of the registered programs.

WHO ARE THE <u>PEOPLE</u> YOU ARE DEALING WITH?

Q: What is the history of the sponsoring organization?

C: The sponsor's company may be relatively new, but the people involved may have extensive and successful oil experience.

Q: What are the backgrounds of all management personnel?

C: The background of technical personnel particularly should be in the areas of interest.

Q: What has been the recent experience of the company in the areas of interest?

C: You should be investing with a firm that has had not only recent, but good experience in the areas to be drilled. There is tremendous variety of opportunity and risk in varying geographical areas. Here again, don't pioneer.

Q: What is the sponsor's financial condition?

C: If the sponsor is obligated for a portion of the program costs—completion costs, for example—does the company's financial condition appear adequate to meet this obligation? In this case, the relative liquidity of the balance sheet may be important. Some smaller sponsors carry on their balance sheets unaudited figures for amounts "receivable from prior programs." These might be only the company's share of a promotional interest that has been estimated in-house and is not the result of an engineering study. Often, the sponsoring company has a fairly minimal balance sheet and has an individual general partner whose net worth is "substantial," or is stated in the offering document. When you call on a sponsor or have a representative do this, you should question the individual general partner about this.

Q: Will an experienced and recognized accounting firm be used?

C: Not necessarily a big eight firm, but one which has had long experience not only with oil accounting, but also with accounting needed with public and semi-public offerings.

Q: How long has the sponsor used the current auditors?

C: A change in auditors occasionally probably means only that the sponsor and the auditing firm might have outgrown each other. On the other hand, in most of the recent scandals in oil involving investor abuse, there was frequent change of auditors. The reasons for change were that the auditor refused to certify the audit without qualification, or it did not feel that the internal accounting of the firm was carried out well, or it did not feel that certain items taken as deductions would hold up. If the sponsor has trouble keeping the same auditor, this is a red flag and you might do well to look elsewhere.

Q: Has the IRS disallowed any deductions of past programs?

C: If it has, it may be back for another look at later programs. (You can find this out by asking the auditors.)

Q: How long has the sponsor had a banking relationship at the bank or banks he uses as references?

C: Stability of banking relationships can only be a plus.

Q: What references outside the oil industry does the sponsor have?

C: By now, you know about the attorneys, the auditors and the banks. Other references would have included suppliers and other oil firms the sponsor had worked with. *Other* substantial citizens can corroborate the character of management, if available.

Q: Have you had enough references checked to satisfy you that further checking would be redundant?

C: The best way to check references is through an intermediary. Have your banker check out the sponsor's bank. Is it an "oil bank"—does it have an oil department? Have your attorney check out their attorney. He will likely use the Martindale-Hubbell directory, which will indicate the firms who have retained the attorneys. An absence of oil operators would be suspicious. Have your tax accountants inquire about the auditors for the sponsor. During these inquiries would be a good time to get the names of technical personnel in the area known to be experienced and reliable. They will be of assistance in helping to evaluate the place.

WHAT QUESTIONS SHOULD BE ANSWERED ABOUT THE <u>PLACE</u> THAT THE PROGRAM IS IN?

Q: Will the programs be concentrated in a particular area or state?

C: While diversification is desirable, it is better in smaller offerings to have some concentration of efforts in areas that are well known. Most 146 offerings do not make widespread drilling efforts, but tend to stay in a limited territory.

Q: What is the nature of oil exploration and development in the area?

C: Some areas are more predictable than others. Some are predictable in their unpredictability. That is, the nature of the area is that there are lots of small pockets of oil or gas not big enough to give reliable surface information from seismic or the like. In these cases, you drill and hope. Other areas by their nature make it unlikely that an unproductive well will be drilled. However, what are the probabilities of drilling economically successful wells? This question could be answered best by an independent

geological consultant whose name you might get when you have the banking inquiry made. It is important that this consultant be an entirely independent evaluator, and not one who makes his living packaging deals to
be drilled. There is nothing wrong with this type of consultant, but you
need in this case, an evaluator and not a salesman.

Q: How about availability of leases in the area of interest?
C: Is it a hot area with rapidly rising prices? Are both cash bonuses and
overrides going up? Is it an area which is dominated by a major company or
a few majors, so that only farm outs are available? These questions could be
answered by a landman whose reputation is also known at the bank of inquiry. Some price comparison of acreage nearby where the program plans
to drill could be enlightening.

Q: What major oil companies are active in the area? Has their activity
shown any marked decrease?
C: Nearly every oil productive area has shown an increase since the
1973 OPEC price increase. Any marked increase in activity over the norm
might indicate tough competition for both leases and drilling rigs.

Q: Are the prices being paid for the leases in line with the other
acreage nearby?
C: Unless a stated part of the sponsor's compensation is profiting on
leases sold to the partnership, prices, both cash bonuses and overrides,
should be competitive. The landman mentioned above can substantiate
this from his records.

Q: Are there any specific problems in drilling in the areas of interest?
C: Some areas present problems in drilling which can run the cost over
the budget. If so, is there a reserve for such contingencies?

Q: Is the sponsor also the operator of the drilling rig?
C: Whoever is to drill the wells, the price should be generally competitive in the area.

Q: Is the contract to be turnkeyed, drilled on a footage basis, or will
there be a charge per day?

C: If the drilling is to be done by a third party contractor at competitive pricing, then this is no problem. Whoever drills the well is entitled to a profit, but not one which is out of line. Many 146 offerings which appear very fair as to structure lose their fairness in too-high drilling contract prices. This should be checked in the area because the price of drilling is the major expense. If this expense is too high, it will have a quite negative effect on return on investment.

Q: Have companies affiliated with the sponsor agreed to sell supplies or services to the partnership, and if so, at competitive prices?
C: Everyone is entitled to a fair, but competitive, profit.

Q: Who will operate the wells?
C: If the sponsor will operate the wells, his field staff should be able to handle this.

Q: If someone else is to operate the wells, does the sponsor charge an additional monitoring fee for this?
C: This can be a double charge. The cost of monitoring should be only a fraction of the cost of operating the wells. Ideally, the operator should operate and monitor the wells. However, a reasonable monitoring charge is not burden enough to foul up an otherwise fair program.

Q: Does the sponsor expect to generate his own prospects: that is, utilize his own geologists' ideas?
C: If a sponsor generates his own prospect and sells a portion of it to an investor partnership on a "third for a quarter" basis, the investors are "promoted" for a 25 percent interest. (They pay all the cost of the well, and get three quarters of the revenue.)

Q: Will the sponsor buy all the prospects to be drilled from third parties?
C: If this is the case, the investors are subjected to a double promotion if both the sponsor and the third party receive a 25 percent promotional interest. In this case, the investors have a 56.25 percent revenue interest ($.75 \times .75$) in the prospect with double promotion. This contrasts with the 75 percent interest in the internally generated prospect. The reason for buying an interest in a prospect from a third party is to be able to buy a

number of small pieces. The double promotion is the price paid for diversification. It allows a small operator to give more diversification than he otherwise could. Most operators originate some prospects and sell off pieces to others from who they also buy pieces of what the others originated.

Q: Will the prospects be farm outs, and if so, are the terms in line with what is being paid in the area?

C: Some areas have much of the available acreage tied up by major companies or independents whose budgets will not allow them to drill up this acreage. Rather than let the leases expire, the owners of the drilling rights will permit a "farm in" on the acreage in return for a percentage of a successful well. In a hot area, this allows the small operator to acquire the right to drill without cash outlay for the acreage.

Q: If the acreage is owned by the sponsor, will it be passed on to the investors at cost?

C: Cost will normally include brokerage fee paid if the acreage were bought through a landman, title expense, and sometimes the interest cost of short term lease ownership before it is passed on to the partnership. Some prospects include the cost of seismic investigation, which should be spelled out in the offering document. The partnership should not agree to pay the cost of seismic unless the lease will be assigned to the partnership.

Q: If the acreage owned by the sponsor is to be contributed to the partnership in return for an interest in the partnership, is the trade a fair one?

C: An unfair trade would be one in which the bonus cost of acreage amounting to $2,500 is contributed for a five percent interest in an $875,000 offering. If there is a trade, the price of the acreage should be stated.

WHAT IS THE PROGRAM STRUCTURE?

Here you will find checklists of considerations which vary depending on your investment preferences, such as: Tax avoidance, or high risk/high potential orientation, or low risk/limited return posture.

Checklist of Key Points if Tax Avoidance is of Paramount Importance

Use a letter of credit at expense of future potential.

This type of program can be used to achieve in excess of 100 percent of the cash invested the first year, but does have numerous pitfalls. These pitfalls were covered in Chapter 3.

☐ 1. Is the letter of credit for a long enough period to permit the completion of all wells in time to establish a history of flow and production which will make the bank comfortable?

☐ 2. Is the engineering firm which has been engaged to do the reserve study for the bank known to the bank?

☐ 3. Does the bank appear willing to make a non-recourse loan at the expiration of the letter of credit of an amount sufficient to release the letters of credit?

☐ 4. How much in the way of proven reserves does the bank want to see to make this loan?

☐ 5. Does the operator have a record of finding enough oil or gas that the bank's reserve or production needs for the loan appear possible?

☐ 6. If the program is not successful, would having your letter of credit drawn upon without any significant tax deduction work a hardship on you? If the primary purpose of making this investment is to avoid taxes in this year particularly (knowing that your tax bracket will drop in subsequent years) this would not be as damaging.

☐ 7. If the amount of the loan is sufficient to allow release of the letters of credit, but needs all the production revenues to amortize the loan, will this "phantom income" (taxable income without corresponding cash distribution) be acceptable to your tax planning?

☐ 8. Are you sure the amount of income tax you are avoiding would otherwise be taxed at 70 percent?

Checklist of Key Points if Tax Avoidance is of Primary Concern

This type of program attempts to provide a valid write-off as close to 100 percent as possible. This is done by having someone else pay all the costs of offering, the sales commission and the capital (non-currently-deductible) costs.

☐ 1. Is the front end cost (offering and sales expense) paid by a third party? If so, what promotion is being given for this contribution?

☐ 2. Is the front end cost being borrowed?

☐ 3. If borrowed, what is the interest rate charged to the investors?

☐ 4. Is the front end cost being actually paid by the sponsor and recouped in the form of a management fee? If so, it will probably not pass IRS scrutiny and could subject the investors to a disallowance of the deductibility of the management fee.

☐ 5. Are capital costs being put up by a third party? What is the promotional cost of this?

☐ 6. Are capital costs being supplied by the sponsor, and what promotion is he taking for this?

☐ 7. Are capital costs being borrowed? At what interest rate?

☐ 8. If capital costs are borrowed, may they be repaid from no more than one-half the net revenue to the investor to avoid phantom income?

Checklist of Key Points if the Investment Has a High Risk/High Potential Orientation

This involves exploration which means that the numerical majority of programs will not get the investors' money back. In successful programs, the return should be several times the investment to make up for the programs which did not pay out.

☐   1.   Does the sponsor have any money at risk?

☐   2.   Will activity be in an area of known recent substantial discoveries of adequate size, if successful, to provide a large return?

☐   3.   Does the sponsor control enough acreage surrounding the high risk prospect so that the investors (and not adjacent landowners) will benefit from development of a discovery?

☐   4.   Has conflict of interest been designed out of the program? The sponsor should not own adjacent acreage without agreeing to give the right of first refusal to the risk-taking investors in case of a discovery. Likewise, if the sponsor has other drilling activities than the partnership, he should agree to no activity in the vicinity to the same depth during the partnership's active efforts. Most sponsors agree to this if they have other activities. It costs little to include this proviso in the partnership papers, and is a protection for investors which should go without saying, but doesn't always.

☐   5.   If the sponsor originates his own prospects, has he any record of selling participations to large independents or major companies active in the area? Bigness is no assurance of success, but the larger companies tend to concentrate their efforts where the big potentials (and the high risks) are. If they are investing with your sponsor, the prospects are likely in "elephant territory."

☐   6.   If prospects are being bought outside, are they being purchased from a major company or large independent?

☐   7.   If acreage for drilling is acquired by farm out, are the terms competitive in the area?

What If the Investment Has A
Low Risk/Limited Return
Posture?

Prior to the price increase which started in 1973 following the Arab oil embargo, the low risk program was not economically attractive in most cases. With the price of oil up nearly 800 percent, they have once again become tempting to many investors who would not go into oil at all. All low risk programs are drilled on proven or semi-proven acreage, which means that reserves will be limited largely to drainage of the well site. These "little wells" are not attractive to major companies who must not commit their capital to prospects with large potential to replace their depleting reserves. Second, many of these little wells produce as "stripper" wells (ten barrels or less per day). Such stripper oil is commanding a price of $40 plus per barrel currently. This stripper price is up from about $18 earlier in 1979. Drilling costs have been increasing on the order of 15–20 percent per year, so the stripper price increase makes the economics more attractive right now than they will be in three years (unless there is another price increase).

Here is an example of how to put a pencil to a low risk drilling venture:

Our example will be a five well package on acreage which has been farmed out by a pipeline company. The total cost of the package is $700,000, including front end costs and turnkey drilling contracts. The pipeline company agreed to allow the original landowner a 12½ percent royalty, but does not have the money to drill the acreage before the lease runs out. It has farmed out the acreage to the sponsor for a cash bonus and has retained for itself a 3½ percent override on production.

The sponsor, who will act as general partner, will take a one percent interest in the program and will share revenues 90 percent to the limited partners before payout, and 80 percent after payout. Payout is defind as total return of capital, in this case, $700,000. An offering this small would have to be a Rule 146 exemption, just to cover front end costs. This is not a recommendation, just an example whose size is kept small so the size of numbers does not overwhelm.

It is assumed that everything checks out as fair in this hypothetical deal. Here is how you might make an informed estimate of the potential worth of this program, if you have good input to feed it. In this case, these proven wells are in an area which averages producing about 15,000 barrels per well. Our estimate will include a selling price of $30 per barrel. Like any other example, this is only as good as the information which goes into it. For example, if the oil recovered is 10,000 barrels per well, the program will not achieve payout. Here are the calculations:

15,000 barrels recoverable per well
$\times$ $30 = total revenues per well of $450,000
$\times$ five wells = total program revenues of $2,250,000.

$2,250,000	Total Revenues
360,000	− 16 percent Lease Burden
$1,890,000	= Gross Revenues
378,000	− 20 percent Operating Expenses
$1,412,000	= Net Partnership Revenues

$1,412,000 $\times$ .90 (to Payout) = $ 700,000.
   642,000 $\times$ .80   =   513,600.

Investor Net Income $1,213,600.

$513,600 ÷ $700,000 = 73 percent Return on Investment

If paid out over ten years—7.3 percent simple annual return

If paid out over five years—14.6 percent simple annual return

Two possible payout periods are given to indicate that the return on investment is directly linked to the time of distribution. Many oil men tend to talk about "two for one" or "three for one" returns, and do not mention the time frame involved. Do not let yourself be misled.

Many snafus can develop even in the "safest" oil ventures. If, for instance, the wells turn out to be gas wells, is there a gathering system near enough to make hooking them up economical? If there is the need for a pipeline, has its cost been budgeted? Even if there is a pipeline nearby, does it have the capacity to transport your gas? These are other points which should be checked before investing.

Do not try to guesstimate the potential value of an exploratory program using the calculations applied to the development wells above. Even if you have access to the geologists' estimates of potential recoverable oil, even a fraction of this potential will give you a paper return so large that you will have fleeting thoughts of mortgaging your home to get into the deal. The reason is that the potential reserves must be relatively large to make up for the majority of dry holes that are a part of all exploratory programs.

If you have invested in an exploratory program, and are given reliable independent engineering estimates, you are now equipped to calculate the revenues due the investors. The time factor cannot be cranked in here unless you have decline curves on productive wells, so the best you can do with no figure except recoverable barrels is to estimate total return.

HOW CAN YOU RATE <u>PERFORMANCE?</u>

Evaluating oil and gas ventures is easy, once the properties have been fully produced. The total return is divided by the investment, and reduced by the time value of money for the period of time it took to produce these returns. The formula for evaluating past performance is simple:

For Cash Return

$$\frac{\text{Cash return}}{\text{Original investment}} = \text{cash return in \% (divide by years for simple annual return)}$$

(OR)

For Present Worth of future net revenues

$$\frac{\text{PWFNR}}{\text{Original investment}} = \text{return on investment (divide by years for simple annual return)}$$

But you cannot invest in depleted properties. You can only make a judgment as to the ability of the operator or sponsor based on his past performance. Performance documentation is indicated by cash distributed to investors or by independent engineering reports from which you can calculate your return. (If there is a liquidation provision, this will be done for you.) Any other figures you get are not meaningful except for the possible effect of reasonable price increases on unproduced reserves.

The purpose of this section of the chapter is to keep you from allowing yourself to be misled by not knowing how the oil business works. When I first got into the investment business, I was approached by an old high school buddy who tried to sell me a whole life insurance policy as a good investment. He pointed out that by paying $10,000 in premiums, I would have a policy worth double what it cost! He quickly left after I pointed out that the forty-year pay-in made this a 2½ percent annual return. He has since become a very successful golf pro.

Following are some examples of statements made by reputable oil people which, taken in context, are the absolute documentable truth. If you don't know the background from which they speak, you could be in a position to misjudge what they are saying. Do these remind you of comments you have heard?

"ABC is a whiz-bang oil operator. He told me for a fact that they could double their earnings next year if they wanted to."

Comment: This company is plowing almost all its earnings back into drilling and thereby, is minimizing its tax bill. It is also creating future reserves to replace those which it is producing. Sure, they could double earnings by stopping exploration, but then they would be a company in liquidation.

"I'm glad you asked about track record! Let me tell you about our 1976 program—only three million dollars. The Bayou Bleu prospect alone, could pay it out. We had a good discovery, good acreage position, and drilled four development wells and found maybe, two or three *billion* cubic feet of gas."

In many businesses, when a direct question is asked, the answer comes out in generalities. There is a tendency in the oil business to lapse into specifics, like the above. The question was not about the best prospect drilled lately, it was about the track record in general, including dry holes. Also, the oil business is one of big numbers, and they get even bigger when you are talking natural gas. A billion cubic feet of natural gas is worth $2,000,000 at $2.00 per MCF, so the Bayou Bleu prospect *was* a good discovery. But the dollars are only gross revenues. You don't know what the lease burden was, you don't know what the revenue sharing arrangement was, and cannot translate this into return on investment with these gross dollars.

"I have drilled over two hundred wells, and never had a dry hole."

By now, you know you are going to get a pitch on success ratio. Completing wells as producers *is* important, but to you the key is what economic return has been produced in either distributable dollars or proven reserves.

"My successful wells have never failed to pay out in less than five years." This is the kind of comment you might hear from an operator or drilling contractor who is being used by an investment partnership.

The first question you should have asked, is about how many of total wells have been economically successful, and then you need to know what he means by "payout." If he is acting solely as operator, payout to him may mean the distribution of sufficient net revenues to the partnership to cover the cost of successful wells only. How about front end cost, management fees, and that portion of the revenues which goes to the sponsor/general partner? The pie has to be sliced up, and this guy is only offering the crust and very little filling.

"Sure, it's risky, but they are only tax dollars."

There are two things no potential investor should ever do: 1) take his checkbook up in a promoter's private jet, and 2) evaluate oil investments in terms of tax dollars only. Just as surely as the investor's eyes will glaze over before the jet trip is over (and the check written before the return landing), the potential investor who thinks of his investment dollars only in terms of tax deductions is far out, also. If an investor wants only tax deductions, he should make a contribution to his favorite recognized charity—that will give a 100 percent write-off, and if it's big enough, might even be worth a bronze plaque!

Tax deductions are an important part of oil investment, but without the expectation of economic return, as stated several times previously, are not sufficient reason alone to invest in oil and gas ventures. (One wag commented that once you have written a check to the IRS, the only way you can get it back is by going on welfare!)

Summary: Checklist of Checklists

In summary, only by being fully informed can you avoid making errors of omission which will cost you money. The scrutiny to which you may subject an oil investment will take some time, and will cost a little money. But if you are considering an investment of $25,000 or more, make the calls yourself, or hire someone to do it.

Here's a 12-point checklist for checking out the preliminaries:

- ☐ 1. Past history of sponsor—documentation adequacy—
- ☐ 2. Past investor communications including tax reports—
- ☐ 3. Sponsor's financial condition—
- ☐ 4. Sponsor's auditors—qualifications and length of relationship—
- ☐ 5. Sponsor's attorneys—
- ☐ 6. IRS problems?
- ☐ 7. References—make phone calls yourself—
- ☐ 8. Prospects' lease costs—get name of reliable landman from local bank.
- ☐ 9. Potential of the prospects—retain local geological consultant—get name form local bank.
- ☐ 10. Who owns drilling rig? Are prices competitive? Telephone check local association of drilling contractors to verify.
- ☐ 11. Is the structure fair? Is all compensation clearly spelled out in the offering document?
  - a. If borrowed money is involved, how will it be paid back?
  - b. Are there any hidden confllicts of interest?
- ☐ 12. What is your gut reaction after meeting the sponsor/operator/manager?

6

Where the Scoreboard Is and How to Read It

Once you have made an investment in an oil or gas venture, finding out where your investment stands will present some problems. First, because of the time needed to drill and develop the properties, there will be a considerable time lag between your initial investment and either a receipt of a cash disbursement or the results of an engineering study. In the interim, you will receive information which may not inform you as it should because you are not sufficiently familiar with the jargon of the oil investment business.

The engineering report can, however, be your most valuable investment tool. It gives you concrete evidence that either you have made a good investment or that you have effected a substantial tax savings—hopefully, both! This chapter will first show you the kind of information you can expect the first year and thereafter. Next, you will be shown how to read and what to look for in an engineering report.

WHAT YOU CAN EXPECT IN THE WAY OF FIRST YEAR INFORMATION

Most oil and gas drilling programs do not hold forth the prospect of any first year return other than tax deductions. If the program is exploratory, it will take two or three years to develop any discoveries and this development will likely utilize early production revenues. If the exploratory program is non-assessable and depends on borrowed funds to pay for the capital completion costs, then these borrowed funds must be repaid with some of the production net revenues, which will slow up or diminish cash distributions. Even in a program which carries an assessment for completion and development costs, early cash distributions are unlikely. Giving out some cash and assessing the investor for a greater amount is trading dollars and amounts not only to window dressing, but is poor cash utilization.

In more development-oriented, or balanced, programs, some earlier cash distributions should be possible. Most balanced programs which stress their ability to get out early cash distributions where "early" means sometime in the second year.

Below will be the sequence in which you will receive your information for tax purposes.

You should receive an early estimate as to the percentage of deductibility sometime in late January or early February. You should receive an IRS Form 1065 for the partnership as a whole, and a Form K-1 for your participation in late March. Some operators do get final figures out of their investors sooner than this, but they are the exception rather than the rule.

The reason for this is mainly that limited partnerships do not operate all their own wells. The majority of sponsors contract out the drilling of wells and must rely on one or more drilling contractors to get the breakdown of intangible and capital costs. When the partnership has bought an interest in someone else's well or wells, the sponsor is dependent on the other operator who may in turn be dependent on *his* drilling contractors for information. After all the information has been gathered, usually the information is given to the auditors for the partnership for verification. This way, final figures given to the investors will not be subject to later revision, which would require subsequent refiling and penalty expense.

Many sponsors will give lip service to providing early information, but it is rare. Do not plan to file early if you are expecting deductions from oil or gas investment. This is not a criticism of the sponsors, but a warning to you of the fact which prevails.

THE TYPE OF PROGRESS REPORTS YOU WILL RECEIVE—EXAMPLES

Aside from tax information, the progress reports which will be sent periodically to investors will be similar for both SEC registered programs and Rule 146 offerings. Although private placements are not generally recommended for individual investors, you should at least be aware of the type of joint venture reporting made available for these programs.

Somewhat surprising to most people is the fact that an investor of $5,000 in an SEC registered program will probably receive more understandable information than the investor of $500,000 in a private placement with a major independent operator. The reasons for this are several. The SEC registered program is designed for the investor who is willing to pay up to a 20 percent premium for a substantial general partner and for diversification. He is additionally willing to pay (either in the form of fees or expense reimbursement to the general partner) for either an individual or a staff to tell him exactly what is going on with his investment. These communications, which should be couched in non-technical terms, will probably be monthly during the period of active exploration, diminishing to quarterly or even annually after all the properties have been developed and put on production.

Investors in Rule 146 offerings will receive communications similar to what is sent out from SEC registered programs. The frequency of reports will vary with the provisions of the partnership agreement. Some 146 sponsors send out Western Union mailgrams since they are dealing with a smaller number of investors.

Private placement investors may be involved in a joint venture. As joint venturers, they may exercise some degree of control over their participation. The operator will send out to each venturer information and a form called an authority for expenditure (AFE). If for some reason the joint venturer chooses not to sign the AFE, then he does not participate in that particular venture. If a joint venturer chooses to exercise this power of choice, then he, someone on his staff, or an expert retained by him for evaluation, will need rather complete information on each project. Most venturers do not permit non-consent without penalty on "required" wells, which are usually exploratory wells. For this reason, the technical information provided joint venturers is far more voluminous, technical and detailed.

Below is a comparison chart showing what information a public investor and a private investor might expect to receive:

Public investor—limited partner	*Private investor—joint venturer*
1. Welcome letter; basically P.R., from the General Partner outlining plans for the year.	1. Welcome letter usually accompanied by prospect reports and AFE's.
2. Monthly communication during the period of active exploration. These will be in non-technical terms and with easily understandable explanations.	2. Daily drilling reports, with either monthly or quarterly summaries of the venture's progress in narrative form.
3. Audited annual balance sheet and income/loss statement for partnership.	3. Continuing flow of new prospect reports on exploratory wells. Reports on prospective development wells with AFE's to be signed.
4. Tax reports as soon as possible after calendar year end.	4. Audited annual statements of the venture with balance sheet and income/loss statement.
5. After two or three years, engineering and reserve studies on productive properties.	5. Tax reports (deductions in the early years) as soon after the first of the year as possible.
6. In a successful program, after a few years, cash distributions from the sale of oil and gas.	6. Certain engineering reports and reserve studies on discoveries and prospective development wells.
	7. In a successful program, after two to three years, cash distributions from the sale of oil and gas.

Following are some actual investor reports:

Here is a sample monthly report from an SEC registered program which is primarily involved in exploration.

Following is a copy of a report to investors in a Rule 146 exemption private placement marketed by E.F. Hutton & Co., Inc. You may note that this is more technical and terse than the report to the limited partners in the Canadian American Fund report. Most investors in 146 exemptions are acquainted with the sponsor on a first name basis and so can call to ask questions. In a widely marketed SEC registered drilling program, with several hundred or more partners added each year, this is not practical.

**Gulfstream
Petroleum
Corporation**

April 16, 1980

Dear Limited Partners:

It is with a great deal of pleasure that we enclose the first Production Report of the 1979-A Drilling program.

These numbers represent revenues from the sale of oil and gas during a partial month from the first two properties to be put on production. Our drilling program is now essentially complete with the last two wells approaching total depth.

You will now be furnished Production Sales Reports on a monthly basis and we hope and trust that these will meet with your expectations as additional wells are added.

Yours sincerely,

FRED D. WARD
President

df

Enclosures

(Includes only those wells which have had a change
in status from Report No. 11)

Gulfstream No. 1 Walton
Newcastle Prospect
McClain County, Oklahoma

Transferred to Production Report.

Gulfstream No. 1-12 Schwind
South Ringwood Prospect
Major County, Oklahoma

Flowing oil and frac water with tubing pressure of 200-250 psi.

Gulfstream No. 1-16 Kennedy
East Rusk Prospect
Major County, Oklahoma

Reached total depth of 8,166 feet on 3-29, ran electric logs. Ran 4½" casing
on 3-30. Appears productive in Mississippi and Manning. Waiting on completion unit.

Gulfstream No. 1-28 Midco Development
Tinker Field Prospect
Oklahoma County, Oklahoma

Moved in completion unit on 3-19. Perforated with Vann gun, had light blow,
no fluid to surface. On 3-22 ran swab and found fluid level at 5,000 feet,
swabbed dry, recovered estimated six barrels of fluid, 50% oil. On 3-23
swabbed estimated 10-12 barrels of oil with 10% load water on last two swab
runs. On 3-25 swabbed 12 barrels of oil with no water (total recovery 25
barrels of oil). On 3-28 frac-treated with gelled condensate and 20/40 sand.
Well screened out, apparently tight. On 3-29 swabbed 1,500 feet of oil. On
3-30 swabbed 100% load water. On 4-1 treated with 18 barrels of acid and
swabbed back; ran tracer survey to check perfs and frac. Squeezed and
re-perforated; re-acidized. Swabbed acid water and formation water with
trace of oil. Sand too tight for commercial production. Preparing to pull
casing (salvage). DRY AND ABANDONED.

Gulfstream No. 1-13 Lawrence
Northwest Ames Prospect
Major County, Oklahoma

Swabbing and flowing oil and water. Total oil on hand 115 barrels.

(contd to page 2)

**Gulfstream
Petroleum
Corporation**

Drilling Reports

139

Gulfstream No. 1 Adams
Hitchcock Prospect
Blaine County, Oklahoma

Preparing to frac.

Gulfstream No. 1-14 Broomfield
N.E. Isabella Prospect
Major County, Oklahoma

Transferred to Production Report.

Gulfstream No. 1-33 Scott
N.W. Drummond Prospect
Major County, Oklahoma

Drilling at 7,090 feet.

Gulfstream No. 1-34 Coulter
S.W. Lahoma Prospect
Major County, Oklahoma

Drilling at 7,657 feet.

Gulfstream No. 1-25 Ott
West Ames Prospect
Major County, Oklahoma

Preparing to perforate.

(contd to page 3)

**Gulfstream
Petroleum
Corporation**

Drilling Reports

SUMMARY OF ACTIVITY TO DATE

Oil Wells	2
Gas Wells	2
Gas Condensate Wells	1
Farm Out (Oil)	1
Dry Holes	4
Completing	6
Drilling	2

TOTAL COMPLETIONS	TOTAL DRY	RESULTS PENDING
12	4	2

**Gulfstream
Petroleum
Corporation**

Drilling Reports

This is a sample progress report from a Rule 146 offering which drilled development wells and has completed the drilling phase and is entering into production.

Here is a copy of a report to investors in one of the widely marketed and successful Canadian American Funds. Although the information contained is understandable and complete, it is not so complex as to confuse an investor who is new to oil investment. Most of the SEC registered oil programs send out very good quality communications to their investors.

2500 Fort Worth National Bank Bldg.
Ft. Worth, Texas 76102
(817) 332-3811

Jack C. Fikes, President

Canadian-American Resources Fund Inc.

Can-Am

February 13, 1976

CANADIAN-AMERICAN RESOURCES FUND LIMITED PARTNERSHIP 1973--3

Reference: Progress Report Number Fifteen
            As of February 16, 1976

The workover at the Pineview (Newton Sheep) in Summit County, Utah,
has been completed. We were successful in shutting off the water
production by squeezing off the old perforations and moving up the
hole to perforate a different interval. In doing so, we opened up
several feet of new pay, which was previously untested and which will
probably add recoverable reserves to this well. The Newton Sheep is
currently producing at the rate of 300 barrels of oil per day and
5 barrels of water. This compares to an average of 490 barrels
of oil per day and 650 barrels of water per day prior to this
workover. The difference in production is due primarily to rock
quality at the new perforation. We will continue to produce at
this rate until a water disposal system has been installed, at which
time we will reopen the old perforations, which should increase the
oil production.

The U.P.R.R. #3-2 on the Pineview prospect is drilling ahead below
13,000 feet to test the deep potential formations on this prospect.
We currently anticipate encountering the first possible productive
formation at approximately 16,500 feet. This well has already
penetrated the Twin Creek and Nugget formations and both appear to
be productive. The deeper formations have enormous potential for
your partnership should they prove productive.

The U.P.R.R. #3-3 has recently begun drilling. This is a development
well to test both the Twin Creek and Nugget formations and will
require approximately 120 days to drill and complete. In addition,
Champlin is drilling a development well in the northeast quarter
of section 3 which will further evaluate this field's potential.

Additional interest in this area has been stimulated by an Amoco
discovery 35 miles to the northeast of Pineview, which tested the
Nugget formation at the rate of approximately 6 million cubic feet
of gas per day plus a large amount of condensate. This discovery
further enforces Can-Am/American Quasar's belief in the potential
of this overthrust area.

-1-

143

The Christmas Creek wells in Alberta, Canada, have been placed on production at the combined rate of 3.4 million cubic feet per day. Production performance from these two wells will have a bearing on the drilling of three additional wells on this prospect.

A new well, Moore Federal #1-1, on the North Ross prospect in Converse County, Wyoming, is nearing total depth. We will be logging the well shortly in order to evaluate its potential. The Moore Federal #6-1 on this prospect is under evaluation after testing oil from the Frontier formation. Logs indicate the well could also be productive in the Dakota; however, neither zone appears to be particularly significant at the present time. Woods Petroleum is drilling an east offset in section 5, which will further evaluate this acreage.

A workover on the Browning (Federal #1) in Carbon County, Wyoming, has been completed. The well is producing at the rate of 30 barrels of oil per day, plus .250 million cubic feet of gas per day. Production performance from this well has been disappointing.

Your Partnership's first Repurchase Price will be calculated as of March 31, 1976, and will be posted in late May or early June.

We will continue to report to you as significant changes transpire.

Sincerely,

Jack C. Fikes
President

JCF/rr

CANADIAN-AMERICAN RESOURCES FUND LIMITED PARTNERSHIP 73-3

AS OF FEBRUARY 16, 1976

BUDGET ANALYSIS

TOTAL SUBSCRIPTIONS: $10,207,500*

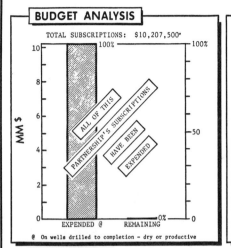

EXPENDED @   REMAINING

@ On wells drilled to completion – dry or productive

STATISTICS

NUMBER OF WELLS:

Completed as producers	13
Attempting to complete/testing	1
Drilling or to be drilled	3
Completed as dry holes	21
TOTAL WELLS TO DATE	38

ECONOMICS

FOR THE FOURTH QUARTER 1975

Lease operating profits net to Partnership – $ 254,000

Cumulative Lease operating profits net to Partnership – $ 1,056,000

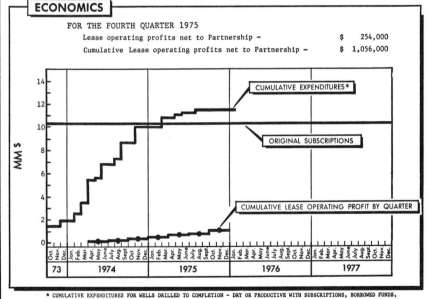

* CUMULATIVE EXPENDITURES FOR WELLS DRILLED TO COMPLETION – DRY OR PRODUCTIVE WITH SUBSCRIPTIONS, BORROWED FUNDS, OR REINVESTED CASH FLOW.

–3–

145

SUMMARY OF DRILLING ACTIVITY
CANADIAN-AMERICAN RESOURCES FUND, INC.
1973-3 LIMITED PARTNERSHIP
AS OF FEBRUARY 16, 1976

STATE OR PROVINCE Prospect/Lease	OPERATOR	COUNTY PARISH OR LOCATION	APPROX. WORKING INTEREST	BUDGETED DRILLING COST - $	APPROX. GROSS ACRES	OBJECTIVE	PROJECTED DEPTH	CURRENT DEPTH	REMARKS
WELLS COMPLETED AS PRODUCERS									
ON-STREAM									
Texas									
Sec. 218/Monroe #3	AQP	Ward	12.49%	185,000	640	Gas	17,500'	TD	Producing 15 MMCFPD.
Mississippi									
Hale/McNeal 4-6	AQP	Clarke	26.25%	90,000	80	Oil	13,500'	TD	Development well. Producing 200 BOPD.
Wyoming									
Browning/Federal #1	AQP	Carbon	18.75%	425,000	3.960	Oil	11,200'	TD	Producing 30 BOPD + .250 MMCFPD.
Utah									
Pineview/Newton Sheep	AQP	Summit	15.75%	730,000	15,360	Oil & Gas	14,500'	TD	Producing 300 BOPD.
Pineview/UPRR #3-1	AQP	Summit	15.75%	330,000		Oil	10,000'	TD	Dual. Producing 800 BOPD.
Alberta									
● Christmas Creek/6-18	QPL		18.00%	67,000	(7,680	Gas	8,700'	TD	} Producing 3.4 MMCFPD.
● Christmas Creek/10/13	QPL		18.00%	30,000	(	Gas	4,400'	TD	
SHUT-IN									
Louisiana									
Bayou Boeuf/Stone #1	Stone	LaFourche	15.00%	171,000	(1,886	Gas	12,500'	TD	Tested 1.7 MMCFPD + 96 BOPD.
Bayou Boeuf/Stone #3	Stone	LaFourche	*	*	(	Gas	12,500'	TD	Tested 3.5 MMCFPD + 120 BOPD.
Wyoming									
No. Ross/Federal 1-31	AQP	Converse	30.00%	440,000	5,440	Oil	14,000'	TD	Tested 270 BOPD.
Alberta									
Branch/Philcan 10-32	QPL		30.00%	68.000	15,360	Gas	4,300'	TD	Shut-in gas well. Tested 2.0 MMCFPD.
British Columbia									
East Grizzly / A-49-H	QPL		15.45%	300,000	(700	Gas	14,000'	TD	Tested 1.4 MMCFPD.
Ojay	QPL		30.00%	1,395,000	18,745	Gas	15,000'	TD	Tested 4.6 MMCFPD.
ATTEMPTING TO COMPLETE/TESTING									
Wyoming									
N. Ross/Moore Fed. #6-1	AQP	Converse	30.00%	700,000		Oil & Gas	14,000'	TD	Under evaluation.
WELLS DRILLING									
Utah									
Pineview/U.P.RR #3-2	AQP	Summit	*	*		Oil & Gas	17,500'	13,307'	Weber test. (Wildcat).
● Pineview/U.P.RR #3-3	AQP	Summit	15.75%	460,000		Oil	10,000'	1,053'	Nugget development well.
Wyoming									
● N. Ross/ Moore Fed. #1-1	AQP	Converse	*	*		Oil & Gas	14,000'	13,612'	Dakota and Frontier development.
DRY HOLES									
Texas									
E. Gem/Henderson 1-65	Mesa	Hemphill	7.31%	105,000	640	Gas	15,900'	TD	Dry & Abandoned.
R.C./S. Strong	Inexco	Culberson	23.33%	390,000	26,880	Gas	17,000'	TD	Dry & Abandoned.
Brownlee Ranch/1-129	Amarillo	Ochiltree	30.00%	205,000	640	Gas	10,800'	TD	Dry & Abandoned.
S. Greasewood/Hermosa #1	ATAPCO	Reeves	3.07%	34,000	640	Gas	17,500'	TD	Dry & Abandoned.
Burton Ranch/2-106	Amarillo	Hemphill	07.50%	160,000	(640	Gas	15,300'	TD	Dry & Abandoned.
Burton Ranch/1-134	Amarillo	Hemphill	07.50%	70,000	(	Gas	15,300'	TD	Dry & Abandoned.
S. Greasewood/Hermosa 2	ATAPCO	Reeves	2.31%	61,000	5,760	Gas	17,500'	TD	Dry & Abandoned.
Louisiana									
Bayou Boeuf/Stone #2	Stone	LaFourche	45.00%	270,000		Oil & Gas	12,000'	TD	Dry & Abandoned.
Gross Isle/E. Moore	AQP	Vermillion	22.50%	385,000	2,400	Gas	14,600'	TD	Dry & Abandoned.
Oklahoma									
South Red Oak/Sutton	AQP	Lattimer	24.00%	677,000	50,000	Gas	14,000'	TD	Dry & Abandoned.
Mississippi									
Boykin Church/USA #21-5	Harris	Smith	26.25%	153,000	2,000	Oil	16,000'	TD	Dry & Abandoned.
Gatesville/Armstrong	AQP	Copiah	30.00%	369,000	4,000	Oil	16,500'	TD	Dry & Abandoned.
S.E.Pontotoc/Dabbs-Mallory	Harris	Pontotoc	12.00%	24,000	3,800	Oil	4,000'	TD	Dry & Abandoned.
Wyoming									
Browning/Federal #2	AQP	Carbon	37.50%	790,000		Oil & Gas	11,200'	TD	Dry & Abandoned. Salt water disposal well.
Alberta									
Fairydell/8-20	QPL		18.00%	20,000	−	Gas	4,100'	TD	Dry & Abandoned.
Iosegun/11-7	QPL		18.00%	50,000	5,120	Oil	8,600'	TD	Dry & Abandoned.
Belloy/10-32	QPL		18.00%	37,000	1,280	Gas	5,400'	TD	Dry & Abandoned.
No. Huile/8-21	QPL		47.49%	191,000	−	Oil	5,900'	TD	Dry & Abandoned.
Branch/Philcan 10-1	QPL		30.00%	57,000	15,360	Gas	4,300'	TD	Dry & Abandoned.
Belloy 7-2	QPL		18.00%	31,000		Gas	5,400'	TD	Dry & Abandoned.
British Columbia									
Oetco	QPL		30.00%	1,500,000	20,000	Gas	14,000'	TD	Dry & Abandoned.

* This well is being drilled on a farmout to another Can-Am program at no cost to your Partnership.

● Changes since last report.

NOTE: (A) The Budgeted Drilling Cost column shown above does not represent actual cost. This figure was estimated from historical data or taken from the AFE (Authority for Expenditure) for the purpose of allocating funds.
(B) The information shown with respect to the various prospects is tentative and subject to change - depending upon completion of all title work, pending trades, rig - equipment - manpower availability versus drilling commitments, etc.

-4-

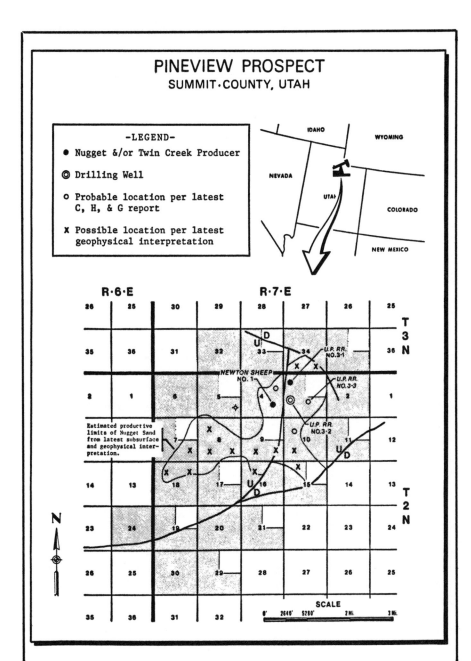

PINEVIEW PROSPECT
SUMMIT·COUNTY, UTAH

-LEGEND-
- Nugget &/or Twin Creek Producer
- ◎ Drilling Well
- ○ Probable location per latest C, H, & G report
- X Possible location per latest geophysical interpretation

147

COMMONLY USED TERMS IN INVESTOR REPORTING

In these reports there will be some terms which are not common to other businesses and for which there is no real translation. Below are some of the more commonly used terms. (Some of these have been used in passing before, but will be repeated for emphasis.)

Prospect Names and Well Names

They are like Morse code, very simple if you know the key.

"Prospects" (usually the acreage block acquired to drill on) are most often named after some nearby identifiable landmark on the location map. This may be a town, railroad station, fire tower, creek, mountain, bayou or prison farm. Thus, you come up with the Love Creek Prospect, the Vinegar Bend Prospect or the Bayou Bleu Prospect.

"Well names" also follow a formula. First, you have the name of the oil company responsible for the drilling (the operator), then the number of the well (number one would indicate a wildcat, or the first well drilled on this acreage by the operator), and last, the name or names of the owners of the acreage on which you are drilling. Usually a county and state location follows the name of the well. Thus, you come up with "The Southeastern Exploration #1 Fatheree, Jasper County, Mississippi," being drilled in the Souinlovey Creek Prospect.

Spud

May be used as a transitive verb or as an adjective. It means the first turn of the bit into the earth. Example: transitive verb, present tense— "We expect to spud the #1 Johnson on April 15." Past tense: "As reported, we spudded five wells during the month of September." Future tense: "We will spud the 33 Bloomfield on June 22." As an adjective: "The tentative spud date for the #1 Smith-Jones is set for December."

Write-Off

Verb, transitive. Write-off—Noun; very, very proper to those in the fifty-percent bracket. Generally, the amount of an investment in oil and gas exploration which is available as a deduction from Federal Income

Taxes. For instance, as a verb: "We presently estimate that the limited partners will be able to write off from 80 to 90 percent of their investment." Or it might be stated, as a noun, like this: "We presently estimate an 80 to 90 percent write-off for the 1979 tax year."

Tax Dollars

That portion of your income which is taxed at fifty percent or more. For a bachelor, this begins at about $32,000 gross adjusted, and for a married couple filing jointly, at about $44,000. Bear in mind that the individual who barely qualifies gets out of the fifty percent bracket as soon as he shelters the first dollar below the aforementioned breakpoints.

Section 263(c) of the Internal Revenue Code of 1954, as Amended

Since 1913, there has been a Federal Income Tax in the United States which has undergone numerous reforms and changes. Through all these modifications, Section 263(c) has remained. Basically, this is the section which states that most of the costs of oil and gas exploration (called intangible costs because they have no salvage value after a well is found to be either dry or productive) are deductible as a business expense against current income. While the intangible drilling cost deduction has remained as a valid deduction against other income, the Tax Reform Act of 1976 did make this deduction an item of tax preference for individuals, but not for corporations.

What this means is that individuals whose tax preference items total $10,000 or half of what would have been their regular tax bill, then to that extent the minimum tax for tax preference items is imposed in the amount of 15 percent. The Reform Act then backtracks and says that in following years if you determine that "X percent" of the intangible deduction was actually attributable to dry holes, then you may file an amended return and get a refund on the minimum tax paid on the documented dry hole intangible drilling costs.

Success Ratio

The total number of wells drilled divided by the number of producing wells resulting. In the past ten years, success rates have ranged from 10 to 20 percent for wildcats drilled, and from 70 to 80 percent for development wells drilled. Success ratios can be very misleading because, after all, it is the amount of oil and gas discovered that produces revenues. A 100 percent success ratio of ten-barrel per day wells which cost $500,000 each can reduce an investor's waistline! Nine dry holes and the discovery of an million barrel oil field is another matter.

Close-In, Offset and Field Wells

Roughly equivalent to development wells. A development well may be "close-in" to a producer, it may be an "offset" drilled adjacent to a discovery well, or it may be drilled in a known field, and so may be called a "field well."

Lost Returns (or Lost Circulation)

The mud which was being pumped down the hole to bring up tailings created by the drilling has been lost. Some empty space below ground has been encountered into which the mud has leaked.

Fracturing

Some traps have good porosity (lots of spaces for hydrocarbons) but poor permeability (the ability of these hydrocarbons to flow out into the well bore). This is often referred to as a "tight" formation. Fracturing—injecting water or oil laden with sand, kerosene or glass beads under pressure—may loosen up a "tight formation."

Coring (or Taking Core Samples)

Core samples may be taken directly out of the well bore or may simply be strained out of the mud which is returned to the surface. These core samples are taken to a laboratory and subjected to microscopic examination and spectrographic and other analyses to determine content.

Formation, Horizon, Pay Zone

All oil and gas production comes from beneath the earth and is contained in a "trap" in rocks or sands which have two characteristics: 1) they have pores in which the hydrocarbons are trapped, and 2) they are permeable so that the hydrocarbons can flow to the earth's surface. Thus, all productive rocks and sands have both "porosity" and "permeability." (Porosity is measured in percentages and permeability is measured in millidarcies.) These productive rocks and sands are layered like a cake and may be referred to as formations, horizons, or pay. "Pay" means to an oil man what "pay dirt" means to a miner.

Fishing

Not a pleasant pastime. When some part of the drilling equipment breaks loose and drops to the bottom of a well which is drilling, then it is necessary to withdraw the drill pipe and use certain special tools to retrieve the object so that drilling may resume. This activity is called "fishing." Can you imagine the difficulty of trying to retrieve an object three miles down in a 7-5/8 inch diameter hole? Bear in mind that all the time you are fishing the cost of the rig, drilling crew and overhead continues. A chartered Rybovich out of Dinner Key or Marina del Rey is considerably less expensive.

Overcall

Many sophisticated investors call the assessability feature of drilling programs by this name. It means the same thing.

Logging

This could be electric logging, gamma ray logging or other types. A logging device is a device which is lowered into the well bore to determine to some degree on the site what may be confirmed by core sampling in the laboratory later.

Casing Point

Often an important determinant in the revenue sharing arrangement. That point at which protective casing is set into the ground to keep the hole from caving in.

Setting Casing

What occurs at the casing point and usually a very encouraging piece of news. This is done after the operator has reviewed logs, core samples and drill stem test results with his geologists and engineers. He has decided that the likelihood of hydrocarbon production in commercial quantities justifies the expense of setting casing to protect the production tubing.

Moving in Completion Rig

The drilling rig is being replaced by a completion rig in order to get the well into production.

Calculated Open Flow Potential

If a large tube—1″ to 2″—were inserted into a reservoir and the oil were allowed to spew out a la "Spindletop" or the gas allowed to flow without restriction, then the flow numbers would be these. In the old days, before reservoir engineering was known or used, the fields then discovered were often produced like this. Often these older fields produced as little as 15 to 20 percent of what reservoir engineers now know is their potential The reason for this is that the reservoir pressure was depleted prematurely due to the open pipe.

This open flow potential is a statistic sometimes used unfairly by promoters to obtain additional funds from investors for development. To use open flow potential as a guideline for future reservoir value is like valuing a farm whose one acre corner on the new expressway has been bought by Exxon for a service station. They paid $100,000 for one acre and the farm is 200 acres, so 200 × $100,000 = WOW! This is patently unrealistic. You should take Exxon's money but keep on plowing. Do not commit to any large expenditure based on open flow potential alone.

Mud

Mud seems to be the catalyst of the exploration industry. They will tell what it does but not really what it is. Mud is a liquid containing any number of chemical and physical ingredients. During the early part of drilling a well, the mud brings up out of the hole the tailings broken loose by the drill bit. While setting production tubing, the weight of the mud equalizes the reservoir pressure until tubing can be set. Mud engineers are the masters of an arcane science and you could get the favorite recipe of a chef at "21" more easily than a mud recipe.

Christmas Tree

A Christmas tree in the oil industry is the productive end of a well. The Christmas tree looks like a plumber's nightmare. It contains all the valves and piping not only to produce, but also to monitor the well.

A Possible Pitfall if the Terms of the Agreement Are Misunderstood

Probably the most difficult for investors to understand is how his percentage changes from spudding a prospect on through production. For instance, if a partnership acquires a 50 percent interest in an operator's interest, and the operator has a 50 percent interest in the prospect, then the partnership has a 25 percent working interest (.50 × .50 = .25 or 25 percent).

Upon commencement of production the lessor of the drilling rights on the acreage begins to draw his overriding royalty interest. Let us say this ORRI is 12.5 percent—an eighth. Now the partnership's 25 percent working interest represents .875 × .50 × .50, or 22 percent in net revenue interest. Let us say that the structure of this deal is that the promoter puts up 25 percent of the risk money and after the investor has gotten back his share of the cost of the successful well, then the operator has earned an additional 25 percent, for a total of 50 percent. The investor's net revenue interest after payout then becomes .875 × .50 × .25, or 11 percent. All of the above changes will have been spelled out in advance, either in partnership papers or in joint venture agreements. The time to understand these terms is before you invest, not after.

ABBREVIATIONS COMMONLY USED IN DAILY DRILLING REPORTS

In addition to the terms of oil reporting with which you need to be familiar, you company may have invested in an oil or gas venture as a joint venturer. In this case you or your oil company will probably be receiving daily drilling reports.

Most daily drilling reports coming into the operator's headquarters will come by telephone or telegram, so brevity means money saved. For this reason, abbreviations are everywhere in drilling reports. It will vary widely from company to company, but here are some commonly used ones. Only by studying the daily reports of an operator over an extended period can you become really familiar with that company's *patois*. On a recent trip to Houston to discuss investor reporting with some operators, I spotted a completely foreign term. Upon querying the treasurer of the company, he admitted that he didn't know what it meant either (but it could have been a typographical error). Here are some commonly used abbreviations:

GIH—going in hole
POOH—pulling out of hole
TD—total depth
PTD—projected total depth
MCF—thousand cubic feet
MMCF—million cubic feet
MCFD—thousand cubic feet per day
BOP—blowout preventer
ITH—in the hole
MW—mud weight
BO—barrels of oil
BOPD—barrels of oil per day
BW—barrels of water
BC—barrels of condensate
POP—putting on pump
P&A—plug and abandon

WHAT THE OPERATOR OR SPONSOR WILL NOT TELL YOU

There are two things which an operator CAN NOT tell any investor. These two things are 1) when a well will be completed and 2) what a property is really worth before it is either fully produced or sold. In the first instance, there are so many variables which go into putting a hole three or four miles into the ground that the time schedule is never a certainty. About the only wells which can be scheduled with any degree of confidence are shallow wells in heavily drilled over areas. Shallow gas wells in areas of West Virginia, Clinton wells in Ohio, the Southern Illinois Basin and the Spraberry in Texas are usually drilled without many unforeseen complications.

Operators drilling fairly deep wildcats just do not know what they may encounter subsurface. For instance, an unexpectedly hard formation down deep may grind up drill bits with distressing rapidity, necessitating pulling out the drill pipe to replace the bit. This is called "tripping." Salt water intrusion may be encountered at lower depths, necessitating protective casing which is expensive and time consuming. The bit may go off center and require that a whipstock make a detour and recenter the hole. The hole can actually collapse or "crater." Most sponsors welcome telephone calls from their investors, but don't waste their time by asking for a firm completion date on a well. When it's complete, they will tell you and they are as anxious as you are to know.

As for the worth of a property, the best estimate can only be had after the field is drilled up to the extent of the trap and put on production. At that juncture, an engineering firm will do a reserve study based on experience (mainly flow and pressure). They will then give an engineering opinion as to the productive potential of the field. Then, at best, their estimate is only an informed guess. Trying to evaluate an oil or gas property before it is produced out is like using a discounted rate of return to evaluate a piece of income producing real estate. The discounted rate of return only becomes real when the property has produced the income and depreciation projected and has been sold. Only after a hydrocarbon property has been fully produced or sold does anyone know what it is worth. Save making this telephone call to the operator or sponsor, too.

FINDING THE BOTTOM LINE

Since no one will know precisely what the value is of producing oil properties, how is it possible to refer to track record with any degree of certainty? The term "track record" should be qualified with an addendum of "to date" unless the properties are either totally depleted or have been sold for cash. (In some few cases, properties have been exchanged for shares of stock. Unless the stock has a firm and broad market, this may not be the best way to liquidate an oil property.)

Track records, or as it usually is labelled in prospectuses, "prior activities" can be shown by three means. The first is the "Investors' Net Cash Table." This shows the amount of money invested in past programs and the amount of cash distributed to investors so far. If, for instance, a program had $2,000,000 invested and had distributed to date $2,200,000, then that program would be 110 percent paid out.

Second, if another program of the same size had completed all drilling activities and then sold all the partnership properties for $3,000,000 cash, then that program would be 150 percent paid out with no more to be expected of it. The first program will go on producing revenues until depletion of the oil or gas.

The third manner of judging track record is using the liquidation value of past programs, if this is something which has been provided. As explained earlier, the formulae for arriving at cash out values are usually very conservative and are subject to high discounts for both the engineering risk and the time value of money. The engineering risk discount is usually 30 to 40 percent of expected future net revenues. The time value of money is usually pegged at 1 to 2 percent over the prime rate. At present, with a prime rate of 13½ percent, this means a discount factor of 14½ to 15½ percent. The result will be that the cash out value will be considerably less than half the ultimate value of production revenues.

To have validity, a liquidation value should be the result of an independent engineering report based on proven reserves. Some programs provide a liquidation value using in-house engineering valuations of not only proven, but also probable and possible reserves. Probable and possible reserves, while they may represent recoverable oil or gas, generally have no loan value at the bank, so these carry less credibility than proven-only figures.

Usually the option to take up a cash liquidation value is accompanied by corresponding figures indicating the expected future net revenues to come from the program. In summary, the report might read:

"The liquidation value of the 1972 program as provided in Section 6 of the Limited Partnership Agreement, is $6,200 for each $10,000 interest in the program. The estimated future net revenues if the interest is held until depletion are approximately $14,000."

What makes the future net revenue estimate probably very low is the almost inevitability of higher oil prices. It would appear that the OPEC nations have adopted the strategy of pricing their oil at just a bit below the cost of alternate sources, and it is likely that this will continue. In mid-1979, when OPEC prices went to $23 per barrel, the cost of producing shale oil was about $25 per barrel. Where the United States is trapped by dependence on foreign oil is that the price increases of this foreign oil also escalate the cost of alternate sources. Until we reduce our dependence on OPEC oil, we will be caught in this dilemma. In light of this pricing situation, it would appear that the value of future net revenues of almost any oil program with an expected production life of five years or more is understated.

For exploratory programs, estimates of liquidation value and future net revenues (usually made after three years) may give a much fairer picture of how the program has done than actual cash distributions. During the first three years, the program may not have distributed any cash because of the need for cash for development.

While this chapter is aimed at helping you understand what is going on with an oil or gas venture in which you may have invested, it also serves once again to underscore two basic premises of oil investment: that it is a long-term investment AND is an illiquid investment outside of the tax savings it may produce until it begins to produce cash.

This book so far, has been concerned with helping the investor and potential investor in oil steer clear of ventures that are likely destined for failure at the outset. It has shown why a great many protections (but no guarantees!) are built into the SEC registered programs and can, with some diggin', be built into a 146 offering. Most of the information given so far has been what experienced investors in oil have found out the long, hard way in the school of experience.

The next chapter will be made up of comments from people of stature in the oil business. Some of their ideas will add many more specific points to the general ideas covered so far.

7

Calculating the Odds for Success

With the more "conventional" investment media, there are numerous ways of cutting down the number of potential spots for commitment of dollars. In real estate, the primary motivation to invest may be tax benefits, cash-on-cash return, long term appreciation, some combination of these and always, location. In the bond market, it is possible to limit investment consideration to certain maturities, yields, or ratings by certain services. In the stock market, one might opt to confine the review of possible purchases to a certain market (over the counter or New York Exchange) with a Standard and Poor quality rating of "X" (or maybe only non-rated "high potential" situations).

In the oil business, there are no such handy criteria. This is one of the primary reasons why the majority of individual investors in oil today choose to put their oil investment dollars into packaged limited partnerships. In these, the sponsors can provide some diversification, the benefit of years of experience in certain prospective areas of exploration and development, and management of all the myriad details that go into the search for oil and gas.

How then can you avoid unnecessary investment risks? What steps can you take to keep from getting into a bad investment? Some techniques to help answer these questions will be given in this chapter.

HOW MUCH RISK ARE YOU WILLING TO ASSUME?

For the serious, substantial investor, either corporate or individual, there are tools available which will indicate very quickly the unsuitability of a potential oil or gas prospect. These same tools may be used for operator evaluation and establishment of a performance index for these operators. For both the individual and the small corporation, these tools are available for self help with a relatively modest investment.

If you have limited demand for information review, and can spend two days' time and between $1,000 and $2,000—the cost of attending a basic seminar on risk management and the cost of a programmable calculator—then you can learn to utilize the techniques to be discussed in this chapter. For the larger investor or small corporation, the same investment in time to attend the seminar, and a total outlay of between $5,000 and $10,000 will pay for the seminar and will buy a microcomputer capable of running numerous risk management programs at a minimal cost of time.

The individual investor leaning toward these advanced techniques should have available at least $200,000 per year for oil investment, and few corporations with an annual budget under $1,000,000 will want to follow the steps outlined below. Next is a brief comparison and contrast between the two types of potential investors.

INDIVIDUAL VS. CORPORATE INVESTORS

Investment by non-oil corporations in oil and gas ventures has been a trend which has become visible in both the annual reports of public companies and in private participations in many areas of exploration and development.

Both individuals and corporations seem largely to take the attitude that the best way to invest is to find a reliable operator whose attitude toward risk is similar to the investor—and then write a check. If there were to be only one criterion for oil investment, the dependability of the person or group running the investment *is* the most important. If only one standard could be imposed, then this—the integrity of oil venture management—should be it.

There are two impedimenta facing the oil investor which many people do not recognize: first, the importance of recognizing one's own ability to withstand risk and, second, the ability to find an operator whose risk aversion level most closely correlates with that of the investor.

Throughout the book we have pointed out a variety of means for avoiding unsuitable investments. The problem with most investors is that they do not have a clearly defined investment goal in mind in approaching oil investment, so that they do not really have the ability to objectively state what qualifies as a suitable investment for them.

The individual investor often wants management and the handling of details to be relegated to someone else, most often because the individual is embroiled in other activities. The individual is usually less risk minded than the corporation. Often, the individual investor does not want the bother or expense of utilizing third party, professional technical advisors. The primary investment motivation of the individual investor is economic, with tax considerations falling second. There is no other valid motivation for individual investment in oil and gas.

The corporation, on the other hand, very often wants some say-so in how its money is being spent. It is often more willing to take larger risks. It is willing to assume the financial and legal liabilities of a joint venture. It can afford and is accustomed to, in the normal course of business, utilizing the services of outside technical consultants. It may well have other incentives than economic return and tax benefits—such as having a call on some of the oil or gas. Finally, since there are stockholders involved, corporate activities must not only be reported, but also documented.

HOW CAN YOU ANALYZE THE DEGREE OF RISK IN AN INVESTMENT?

In both the individual and corporate categories, the investors with some oil investment experience may have a fair idea of investment goals, whereas the inexperienced investors generally do not. For both the inexperienced and the experienced investor who is both serious and sufficiently substantial, there is a tool now available which did not exist twenty years ago. This tool is risk management. Risk management is the application of risk analysis, which utilizes mathematical probabilities and also allows the factoring in of the investor's willingness to assume a certain amount of risk for a certain amount of return.

Four Aspects of Risk Taking

1. Taking unknown chances: Those who risk money on ventures whose outcomes can only be guessed at are usually taking risks they do not even know of.
2. Avoiding unnecessary risks: Most of this book has been directed at showing you how to steer clear of those risks of oil investment which are avoidable.
3. Taking known chances: Most people have a good grasp of what the odds are in their regular line of endeavor. The multifaceted nature of risks in the oil business still leaves many in a state of puzzlement. The first part of this book points out many of the legal and tax risks. The better part of Chapter 5 was spent in assisting the potential investor to investigate risks due to management inadequacies. All this concern occurs before facing the actual risk of drilling for oil or gas.
4. Quantifying known risks: Just where in your investment risk spectrum can one place oil and gas investment? A modest dollar cost and some study time, supplemented by some professional help, can teach you how to quickly cull out those deals which are below your investment standards—either they provide too low a return for the risk involved or the risk is too high for the expected return. This is the function of the application of risk analysis, called risk management, to oil and gas exploration.

The Wisdom to Know the Difference

Before describing the elements of risk management, here are several examples of the misunderstanding of the nature of risk. Mistaken assumptions open the door to invalid conclusions and often cause needless monetary loss.

Example #1: In the late 1960s, a promoter in Mexico advertised for sale, over a Tiajuana radio station, fractional interests in a well he was drilling in the Monterey desert. No production had ever been found in that area. He usually began drilling with very little investor participation. As the well progressed, he coaxed investors into his deal with this pitch given over the SEC-proof radio station:

"Hurry, hurry, hurry! Get your fractional participation in an exciting new wildcat oil well now being drilled near La Trampa. A 1/128th interest will only cost you $3,000, and who knows what it may be worth? This wildcat is going down to 7,000 feet. Well, it's down to 3,500, so half the risk is already gone! Hurry, hurry, hurry . . . . .!" Investors in the U.S. gave this promoter their money for several years. Degree of risk cannot be measured by footage drilled in a single wildcat.

This is a sad example of investors wanting risk measurement to be very simple. They were taking a risk as presented by the promoter which had no relation to real risk.

Example #2: A canny (if unethical) geologist in Jackson, Mississippi, approached a substantial investor with a plan to do some developmental drilling on some proven acreage in a gas-prolific area of Mississippi. The deal involved drilling several close-in wells on proven acreage at a cost of several hundred thousand dollars. The return on investment was estimated at about 2:1 (without tax effect and not discounted to present value). The investor, who was sophisticated, but not knowledgeable of the area to be drilled, made an inquiry of an officer in the oil department of a local bank as to the soundness of the venture. A week later, the bank officer called the potential investor and said, "I have verified the employment history of the geologist, and it is accurate. He has a letter of intent to drill from ABC Co., and they are reputable. The price at which he has optioned the acreage is in line with what is being paid for proven acreage in the area. However, the field in which he intends to drill has actual reserves of less than half the estimate he used to compute expected rate of return. The best you can hope for is to get your money back over a lengthy period. You would probably suffer an economic loss from not having had the use of your money. Steer clear of this deal."

Although the probabilities of completing these close-in wells as producers was high, the likelihood of any real economic return was close to zero. The geologist probably sold the deal at a later date to a less cautious investor.

This investor took the trouble to find out what the known risks were. He decided this did not fit in with his needs. (This deal might have worked out for an investor who was primarily tax-oriented, by using a letter of credit.)

Example #3: A long time friend of mine, a pathologist, called me early during my involvement in oil and gas financing. He had a chance to go in on a single well and with some other medics on his staff, and asked my opinion. I urged him strongly to pass this one up, just because it was a single well, but offered to look at the offering. When I received the document, it was clear that it was a highly promoted well in an area which normally produced gas wells. The nature of production in this area was that they had a very generous flush period but went directly into a rapid decline and depleted very quickly—often in less than two years. I called the doctor, only to find to my dismay that he had already committed some money to this well. I warned him against further investment in this sort of deal. Unfortunately, he invested not only in that one but in several others, basing his expected return on the cash distribution from the short flush periods. He did receive a full tax deduction, and got about 40 percent of his money back before the wells depleted. The initial money he received from the first well's production spoke louder to him at the time than the voice of experience.

Example #4: A former CPA, who was part of a group who had much success in investments, was asked to look at a multiple well deal. The CPA went to visit the promoter in New York, verified the history of the promoter, and had the credentials of the driller checked out. The promoted had had limited experience in oil, but had a clean reputation. The driller, who had packaged the deal for the promoter, had no black marks against him. The CPA went to the site of the proven acreage and retained a geologist to evaluate the information given him by the promoter. The geologist said that the technical information led him to believe that the deal was economically viable, though he had not worked in the close vicinity of the prospective acreage.

The group went into the multi-well deal and all were completed as producers. Unfortunately, the volume of gas was not sufficient to justify running a line the considerable distance to a gas distribution company's line. The only question not answered before investing was the one about availability of economical transporation of the gas. The group assumed that this would not be a problem. Their assumption, that this unnecessary risk was taken care of, cost them money.

Risk Mitigation through Diversification

Diversification is a must for oil and gas investment. It is always better to have ten percent of ten different wells than 100 percent of one, if the wells are equally risky. Admittedly, the successful wells' results are diluted by the unsuccessful ones, but the chances of a total wipeout are reduced.

The degree of diversification depends both on the degree of risk assumed and the comfort level of the investor.

In addition to diversification in number of wells, some diversification in time is desirable, since a given operator can have bad years. I suggest three years' commitment, at least.

What Are The Elements of Risk Analysis?

To apply risk analysis, you must have access to the probabilities of success and failure, and the dollar consequences of success and failure.

Probabilities are expressed in percentages which must always add up to one (.60 + .40 = 1.00). That is, 60 percent chance of success means that the chance of failure must be 40 percent.

The cost of failure in oil and gas drilling can be expressed in terms of dry hole cost. The expected value of success is expressed in expected dollars returned from a successful well.

Most risk analysts express basic risk by using a lottery diagram, like the one below:

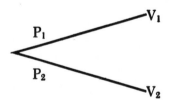

This lottery diagram has two probabilities expressed by P_1 and P_2. There are two values represented by V_1 and V_2. V_1 is negative and indicates a loss, while V_2 is positive and indicates a gain. The lottery diagram can be expressed by a simple equation:

$$(P_1 \times V_1) + (P_2 \times V_2) = \text{Expected Value}$$

The lottery diagram will give an expected value of any risky venture.

HOW RISK MANAGEMENT WORKS

The Toss of a Coin

A lottery diagram for the toss of a coin for $1,000 will look like this:

$$P = \text{Probability} \qquad V = \text{Value}$$

$$P_1 = .50 \qquad V_1 = 0$$

$$P_2 = .50 \qquad V_2 = \$1,000$$

or $\qquad (P_1 \times V_1) + (P_2 \times V_2) = \$500 \text{ E.V.}$

Using the equation $(.50 \times 0) + (.50 \times \$1,000) = \$500$ Expected Value. The Expected Value of a "chance" on this lottery is $500. Some people might toss a coin for $1,000, but almost no one would buy a chance for $500. A promoter, of course, would sell 3,000 $1 chances: 1,500 on heads and 1,500 on tails, and pocket the difference!

Most lottery ticket buyers are not investing, they are having fun or supporting some charity. The difference in the $1 lottery ticket buyer and the one who would actually toss a coin for $1,000 lies in willingness to assume risk.

For example, a starving, naked, homeless person who has only $1,000 to his name would not toss the coin. His $1,000 can buy for him food, clothing and shelter.

On the other hand, a multimillionaire might toss the coin because the outcome might only mean the difference in one or two weekends in Acapulco this year, if even that.

How To Find Your Level of Willingness To Accept Risk

A graph called a utility curve can be plotted for the two extreme cases cited above. The basic assumption of the utility curve is that as wealth increases, the basic value of additional wealth becomes less important and, by the same token, the possible consequences of total loss are less important. The reverse is also true. In plotting a utility curve for the two persons above, put on the vertical scale numbers from 0 up to +10. We can call this their willingness to assume risk. On the horizontal axis, plot from 0 to $1,000. The starving man would put his risk adjusted value at 0. The multimillionaire might put his level all the way up to +10. At some point between 0 and +10 on the graph lies the willingness to assume risk by investors in less extreme circumstances.

The problem with a utility curve is that the results of plotting one give the mathematicians a value which they call a "utile." A utile has no absolute value, only a relationship.

Risk analysis is theoretical until some value is placed on the expected results of the risks taken. To benefit from risk management, an investor, whether corporate or individual, must put himself in a pigeonhole relegated to some degree of risk. Somewhere between the starving, naked, homeless person and the multimillionaire attitude is a degree of willingness to accept risk that will represent you. Another way to express your willingness to accept risk is to call it "risk aversion." What is needed is a measurement of your aversion to risk to apply to an expanded lottery diagram or even to a series of lottery diagrams.

An earlier, cruder method of risk management has been to discount risk at some rate of interest. This does not work satisfactorily in the oil and gas business because of the wide variation of degree of risk in the drilling of a single prospect. For instance, what rate of discount should you use in the drilling of an exploratory well? If drilling is successful, what rate of discount should be applied to the amount needed to complete the well? Once the well is on production, what discount is necessary to give weight to the possibility of cessation of production? Then, how much should the cost to the casing point of development wells on the prospect be discounted? The development wells' completion cost? Production from the development wells?

Even if a percentage discount were agreed upon, would the percentage apply to everyone uniformly, the investor with $200,000 to invest, or the major with $200,000,000? The answer is, "No."

Risk Adjusted Value

What is needed is a risk adjusted value for each risky venture which bears a meaningful relation to the entity putting the money at risk. This risk aversion value could indicate that a venture might be suitable for inclusion in a $4 million budget, but not in a $400,000 annual budget. Or, by the same token, it might indicate that the venture would fit into the plans of one investor with a $400,000 budget, but not fit another with the same number of dollars but a different level of risk aversion.

How Risk Adjusted Value Is Determined

There are two ways of determining risk aversion and assigning to it a useful number. These are by application—of past experience; or by observation—of another's experience.

Caution: Past performance should not be used as the sole indicator of the future in oil and gas investments because the operator may change his attitude toward risk and radically alter the type of prospects he's drilling. The assumption is that an operator has been successful because he has been taking risks commensurate with his ability and willingness to assume the risk. Based on his past experience, if he continues to take the same type of risk (and this should include a fair number of prospects over, say, a five year period), then it is highly likely that his future results will closely parallel his past results. A change in attitude toward risk can bring an even more dramatic change in results, on both the upside or downside.

For the experienced investor, individual or corporate, or the successful operator who wants to find out *how* he has been successful, past history can be used as a benchmark.

No attempt will be made to justify the mathematics of risk management now. If you wish to delve further into the mechanics of how it works, at the end of the chapter there are some specific recommendations for you. The purpose of this section is not to make the reader an expert in risk analysis, but to make him aware that these tools are available. The results of the mathematical logic involved, modified for the particular characteristics of petroleum exploration, can speed up the decision-making process.

Here is a lottery diagram for an exploratory well:

$$P_1 = .20 \qquad V_1 = \$500,000$$

$$P_2 = .80 \qquad V_2 = -\$100,000$$

Other probabilities and values could be added (e.g. just getting the $100,000 back) but let's keep this simple.

The risk adjusted value for this proposed well may be expressed in an equation, as follows:

P = Probability
V = Value
R = Risk Aversion Level

The equation for ariving at a risk adjusted value is:

$$Risk\ Adjusted\ Value\ =\quad -\frac{1}{R}\ In\,(P_1E^{-RV_1} + P_2E^{-RV_2})$$

If the risk adjusted value of this prospect is "0" or negative, it should be rejected unless the operator is willing to assume a different level of risk aversion than has been his historical practice.

But this equation is insoluble without assigning some value to "R." The Wharton School of Business Risk Education has determined by working for years with major oil companies and smaller independents that risk aversion levels may range generally from .000,000,001 (for a large operator with a budget of $100,000,000 or more) to .000,001 (for a small operator with a budget of a few hundred thousand dollars). For purposes of computation, these values may be expressed in scientific notation, or $.01 \times 10^{-6}$ and 1×10^{-6}, respectively. For the above example, an arbitrary R of 1×10^{-6} (or simply 10^{-6}) will be used.

Using the probabilities and values from the lottery diagram in the equation, with an arbitrary R of 10^{-6}, will give a risk adjusted value of $-\$5,248$. For anyone with a risk aversion level of 10^{-6}, this prospect should be rejected.

How Risk Aversion Level is Determined

A Risk Aversion Level can be established for any investor (or operator, because the largest investors in exploration are the oil companies). Reconstruct the record of all wells drilled (or participated in) and then work backward to a zero risk adjusted value. This is the point at which past experience indicates that you have drawn a line. Any risk adjusted value which is negative would have been rejected. The average of risk adjusted values for the period of experience under scrutiny will indicate a risk aversion level. Using your "R" — your particular risk aversion level, in reviewing prospects, any with a negative value should be rejected. If you are an experienced investor, it should entail no more than some digging to come up with the input necessary to give you a risk aversion level based on your investment experience. If you are not sufficiently experienced, then your problem will likely be one of comparing operators to see which one has done the best job for his investors in light of the risks assumed.

How Risk Management Is Used
for Operator Evaluation

For example's sake, let us consider a corporate natural gas end user which is considering direct investment in exploration in order to get call on the gas discovered. Choice of an operator (or operators) on a rational basis is necessary, because the board of directors will want documentation along with recommendations. The choice of operators will be to some degree self-limiting because of:

geography
interstate pipeline service
distribution networks
size of annual investment
operator availability

The list will be culled down to those who have extensive experience in the area to be drilled, those of adequate internal financial strength to carry the program, and a few who are interested in meeting the demands of a non-industry partner. The list will probably be narrowed to a very few after a short while. Then, all other things being equal, how can two or more operators be compared on an accurate, rational and consistent basis?

The competing operators would be asked to supply input for an evaluation for, say, a five year period. This information would include, on all wells drilled for each of the past five years:

1. the probabilities as estimated going in
2. the estimated dry hole costs vs. actual
3. cash flow from successful wells

The risk aversion level of each operator can be calculated using this information.

Then, utilizing the risk aversion level and correlating it mathematically with the cash flow produced for all dollars invested over the period, a discounted return called, "risk adjusted value per dollar budgeted," can be calculated. This will show how large a return was realized for the amount of risk assumed. Then the choice becomes relatively simple.

If two or more operators have had about the same risk aversion level, then the one with the consistently higher return would be the choice. Or, if two or more operators have had about the same risk adjusted return for their efforts, the one with the higher risk aversion level would be chosen.

Finally, if the corporation is joint venturing with the chosen operator, the information gained can be used to evaluate the prospects presented to the joint venturers. Since the operators' risk aversion level becomes yours when you join the venture, if he is not using risk management to evaluate his prospects, you can, using the first equation shown above.

Is all this too good to be true? If you think it's as easy as reading this chapter, you are right. Understanding the uses of risk management is relatively simple. The application of risk management will take a lot of study and a continuing amount of time. But it is being used every day by every major oil company and many independents who need this adjunct to their decision making. The initial investment of time will be sizeable. Once you set up, the amount of time saved in not reviewing unsuitable prospects will be larger every year it is used.

GIGO—Garbage In, Garbage Out

Those of you who have worked with calculators or computers recognize this by-now-timeworn heading. If the input is inaccurate, the output will be inaccurate.

Of the four basic inputs required of risk analysis (two probabilities and two values), only one can be controlled and that is dry hole cost. Some oil men will say that this cannot be controlled. It can, by abandoning the well when the estimated dry hole cost has been expended! The probabilities of success or failure are estimates and become more meaningful as an area is developed.

Verification of probability input can be achieved by using consulting engineers in the area of interest. The numbers supplied by in-house geologists and engineers will probably be optimistic and should be verified outside.

In the area of operator evaluation, a five year study of results would show, because of the presumed further development of areas drilled earlier, the degree of accuracy of the original estimates compared with actual experience in the area during the subsequent five years.

Here's a Note of Caution: beware of computer printouts used as sales tools. One major marketer of an SEC registered program used this in the early 1970s to show how sexy their prospects were. This was illegal, but it raised a lot of money. These printouts had been rigged to show an inordinately high potential return. Printouts might be used with a joint venture, but even then, outside verification is a must. It's either that or buy your oil deals from the computer company!

How To Do It

There are several possible approaches to utilizing risk management as an adjunct to exploration decision making. They are:

— do-it-yourself, using a programmable calculator
— do-it-yourself, using a leased terminal from a computer service bureau

— do-it-yourself, if you are a corporation with a computer set-up in place and personnel qualified to implement programs which can be purchased

— hire it done, using technical consultants who have, or have access to, computers already programmed.

Here are a few names and addresses of computer oriented consultants:

TLR Consultants
Petroleum and Geological Engineers
1117 United National Bank Building
1509 Main Street
Dallas, TX 75201

Hudson Consultants, Inc.
Petroleum Engineers
302 Thompson Building
Tulsa, OK 74103

I. P. Sharp Associates
Suite 1150
183 Main Street, East
Rochester, NY 14604

For the individual who is mathematically inclined, using the programmable calculator for single prospect evaluation is fairly easy to learn, and does not take an undue amount of time. If you are such an individual, who has enough experience in buying pieces of single prospects that you can arrive at a risk aversion level, this probably should be your choice. If you do not look at more than twenty to thirty prospects per year, this is your most economical bet.

If you are a larger individual investor, or are a small operator who needs to review a greater number of prospects than this, you would do well to look into leasing a computer terminal which is plugged into a service company already programmed for oil and gas risk management. There is such a company called PSI Software Inc. located in Houston, Texas (which makes its software available on the General Electric service) which offers a program with the acronym "POGO," for *P*rofitability of *O*il and *G*as *O*perations. The terminal can be placed anywhere convenient to a telephone and can use a service bureau already programmed for prospect evaluation.

If you feel sufficiently knowledgeable of the area under consideration, you may use estimates provided by your operator. Otherwise, you may wish to locate a consulting firm in the area who can verify or modify the estimates given. (Use your bank to get a recommendation from an oil bank in the area of interest, just as suggested in the "due diligence" work in Chapter 5.)

For a several year study of an active operator, say one who has drilled 30 to 50 wells per year, it is almost mandatory that you use a consulting firm with access to a service bureau or in-house computer. The time required to do this on a programmable calculator is too great.

WHAT THE USE OF RISK MANAGEMENT CAN DO FOR YOU

Once you have established a risk aversion level for yourself or for the operator of your choice, you will be able to reject a prospect as unsuitable in about ten minutes, using only the basic input of reasonably accurate estimates of probabilities and values.

You will be able to have made a meaningful comparison of the risk adjusted track records of two or more operators for a five year period. This job can be done in about two weeks after all the data are gathered. Further, an annual updating of the operators' risk aversion level can be made with very little effort and time involved. There are additional applications of the data gathered for basic risk management, but it is not within the scope of this chapter to present them.

HOW MUCH ARE TWO TICKETS ON THE FIFTY?

Some investment in both time and money will be required if you are to be able to use the tools available for the management of oil and gas exploration risk. First, you or your surrogate must be exposed to the basics and then you must become familiar with using these tools. Then you must learn to apply these basics. Finally, you must either have the equipment or have access to the equipment necessary to perform the calculations.

The cost of equipment is modest. A hand held programmable calculator is available for under $250. The same work can be done on a number of "hobby-size" home computers which now sell for under $2,000 with some peripheral equipment.

If you prefer using a computer terminal, this is available on lease for $85 to $100 per month. In addition to telephone charges for connection with a service bureau, there will be a charge for time by the service bureau which can vary rather widely.

For those with a need or desire for having the job done outside by others, there are several firms in various locations in the U.S. and Canada who can provide not only the calculations needed, but also verification of input, since these firms also do petroleum geological and engineering services. The expense of farming out this sort of work can vary widely. As a guideline, a consultant firm like the one described, estimated for me the cost of a five year study for the purpose of operator evaluation. This would have involved input on about 200 wells (average of 40 per year), the calculation of an annual risk aversion level, and an overall five year risk aversion level. The cost was under $5,000. For future prospect evaluation, the cost would be less than $5 per prospect.

With the above package, you could telephone information on a prospect or prospects to the firm, and have an evaluation the same day.

A FINAL WORD

Risk Management is not a panacea for the problems of decision making. It is a valuable adjunct to making decisions. It cannot point out the good deals, but, given the proper input, can indicate very quickly that a proposed investment is not for you.

In the final analysis, the great speed and scanning ability of even the programmable calculator gives the decision maker, whether corporate or individual, a degree of guidance which cannot be achieved for a similar output of time and money by other means. It cannot take the place of human judgment, but can give accurate, consistent and rational assistance in making this judgment more profitable.

For anyone who is seriously interested in learning the basics of risk management the leading institution in the field of oil and gas risk management is the School of Business Risk Education, a part of the Wharton Business School of the University of Pennsylvania.

The Director of this School, Dr. John Cozzolino, gives an intensive two day seminar in major metropolitan centers in the United States and some other countries, periodically.

For those who have had some experience with sophisticated hand held programmable calculators, Dr. Cozzolino has published a book with the same title as the seminar, *Management of Oil and Gas Exploration Risk,* based largely on the material presented in the seminar. The book is aimed at persons who are into fairly advanced mathematics (beyond the undergraduate level). There is a Level Two advanced seminar in oil and gas risk management for those who have completed the basic seminar.

RISK MANAGEMENT IN PERSONAL FINANCIAL PLANNING

The foregoing material is so highly mathematical that my editor felt that some more subjective criteria for readers interested in the risk aspects of oil investment would be of value. Bear in mind that the basic premise of this book is that the first step in making a good investment is avoiding a bad one or one which is unsuitable to your personal financial situation at the time.

Since it is unlikely that any reader of this book is in either situation dreamed up for the hypothetical "toss of a coin for $1,000," here below are two tables to help the average reader (who is neither a starving, naked, homeless person, nor a multimillionaire) arrive at two important decisions: should I play the Energy Investment Game? And, if so, how should I play it?

Should I Play the Energy Investment Game?

The following table does not purport to take into account all the variables which go into making this decision. It does apply a rating to two important criteria, age and gross adjusted income. Please read the explanation and footnotes which follow the table.

The ratings are:

1. Best situation;
2. Acceptable situation;
3. Marginal situation.

Table 1

Gross Adjusted Income/Rating

Age/Rating	Filing Singly	Filing Jointly	
20-60 ①	over $115,000	over $223,000	①
60-70 ② °	$115,000–$37,000	$223,000–$49,000	②
over 70 ③ °	under $37,000	under $49,000	③

Brief explanation: Age criteria should be self explanatory, since most authorities accept that it is preferable to be young and wealthy in any general situation. Specific to oil investment however, are the facts that the "fifty-percent" bracket begins at about $32,000 for those filing singly and at about $44,000 for those filing joingly.

If we assume at least $5000 potential investment in oil, then any unexpected deduction generated late in the year (after the oil investment has been made) *may* mean that gross adjusted income drops below the fifty percent bracket and the investor may not be getting full advantage of the tax incentives provided.

° For the older investor who may consider his situation marginal because of age, oil investment may offer an opportunity to benefit from early tax incentives. Then he can pass on to children, or grandchildren, valuable reserves in the ground at a highly discounted valuation. Most SEC registered programs provide, after two or three years, a liquidating or cash-out value based on an engineering study of reserves. Since, in most cases, both the study and the value are very highly discounted, this valuation may be used for passing on to others this asset, free of gift taxes (up to $3000 per recipient for single donors and up to $6000 per recipient for joint donors). Thus, an older couple with high taxes to pay might put $10,000 into a drilling program which could provide a $10,000 deduction over two years, which would save them $5000 in taxes (a trip to South America is more fun than paying taxes!) Then, in year three, for instance, if future net revenues were determined by the engineering study to be, say, $15,000; then, applying current interest rates (to discount to present value) and *then* applying a 30–40 percent "haircut" for the risk of reserves in the ground, the liquidating or cash out value of this future net revenue might be only $6000. The couple could then give this asset—valued at $6000—free of gift taxes, and feel satisfaction in knowing that the asset will be worth more than this to the recipient, probably a child or grandchild.

How Should I Play The Energy Investment Game?

The ratings are, once again:

1. Best situation;
2. Acceptable situation;
3. Marginal situation.

Table 2

Primary Investment = Goal	Preservation of Capital or	Building equity/ future income or	Capital Gains
Program Type			
Exploratory	3	1–2	1
"Balanced"	2–3	2–1	2–3
Development	1	2	3

This brief addendum provides fairly subjective criteria to assist you in making your decisions. Your final decision will depend on your total personal financial situation and should involve conferences with your tax accountant, tax attorney and broker.

8

Advice for the Big Leaguers

If your firm meets the following qualifications, it has an economic opportunity which has not appeared before in the history of the United States. Here are the qualifications, if your firm:

1. Uses 1,000 MCF (a million cubic feet) of gas per day, and
2. The gas is used for feedstock, or
3. High priority process purposes, and
4. The company can afford to invest upward of $1 million per year, and
5. Believes that natural gas prices will rise; THEN—there is an opportunity to acquire:
   a. an 8-12 year supply of a basic raw material,
   b. at a 25 percent to 75 percent discount from the current market
   c. with no storage charges.

The basic raw material is energy in the form of reserves acquired by direct participation in exploration.

The opportunity is to be a direct participant in such exploration. The incentive for participation is to acquire reserves at big discounts from today's market—a price which will not increase.

Tax benefits and cash profits are not a part of the purpose of such a program but they can accrue under present law.

In this chapter we show you how a firm's program should be organized and controlled. You will find practical tips on what your firm should think about when choosing an operator as well as a checklist of the steps you should take when planning and managing the program.

HOW THE STAGE WAS SET FOR SUCH AN UNUSUAL CORPORATE OPPORTUNITY

Most of the nation's natural gas pipelines were constructed after World War II to bring to the consuming public a formerly almost useless fuel at very competitive prices. The pipelines in interstate commerce were to be regulated by the Federal Power Commission. The FPC had a dual responsibility; both to the consumers and to the pipelines. Consumers had to be given fair prices. The pipelines needed assurance of a rate of return sufficient to pay the large costs of construction.

One thousand cubic feet (an MCF) of natural gas has a BTU equivalent of about one sixth of a barrel of oil. After World War II, oil was still selling at about $3 per barrel. But since natural gas was largely being flared in the field as a nuisance, many of the pipelines signed early contracts for natural gas supply at 10¢ to 15¢ per MCF, well below the oil parity price. Financing for the pipelines was largely based on this low price. Consumers had a clean burning fuel at a price well below either oil or coal equivalents. The pipelines were able to amortize their debt and show a reasonable return to stockholders. Gas prices, therefore, were under little pressure to escalate. By 1970, the posted (regulated, or interstate) price of gas on the Gulf Coast was pegged as low as 17¢ per MCF.

The interstate pipelines began to feel the pinch of competition for gas supply as an interstate market developed for natural gas. The FPC had authority on pricing and transportation in interstate commerce. It had no authority over users in a gas productive state nor over intrastate pipelines. These groups created the intrastate market, which in 1970 was at the 35¢ to 40¢ per MCF level.

In addition to the pipelines' uncompetitive position with regard to replacing reserves by purchase, the pipeline industry had seen, over a twenty year period, a growth in the usage of natural gas which was considerably higher than anticipated. Faced with an unexpected growth in usage, dwindling reserve positions, and locked into an uncompetitive bidding situation, many interstate pipelines began direct participation in exploration for new supplies of gas by several means.

The FPC permitted the pipelines to make advance payments to producers in return for a call on the gas discovered by exploration efforts financed by these payments. These advance payments were added to the pipelines' rate base so that this money could be used in calculating rates and the return on investment by the pipelines.

Second, pipelines began joint venturing with exploration companies. Usually they put up a portion of the money for a venture and received a call on all gas discovered, for which they agreed to pay the highest posted price. There was some problem in finding operators to accept the limitation on price because it did reduce the potential return on investment (because this gas could not be sold in the unregulated intrastate market).

Finally, many of the pipelines began hiring petroleum technologists—geologists and engineers—to assist them in evaluating opportunities in the area of advance payments and joint ventures. These technical staffs, in many cases, formed the nuclei of what have become fully staffed exploration subsidiaries of the pipelines.

Meanwhile, the cost of exploring for and developing additional reserves of natural gas had increased to the point that, in 1971, oil and gas drilling activity dropped to a ten-year low. Fixed prices in the face of escalating costs had taken away much of the incentive to explore.

In 1973, the posted price of natural gas was increased to 52¢ per MCF, and for a brief period, the price of gas was on a parity with oil at $3.12 per barrel. Then, in the autumn of 1973, came the Arab oil embargo and the quadrupling of world oil prices to $12 per barrel.

The End User Whipsaw

Knowing that seasonal demand for natural gas could vary widely, the FPC had devised several categories arranged according to priority and price. The highest priority included homes, hospitals and schools. They got first call on all gas throughout year round. For this "firm" service they paid a higher price.

Next down the list were high priority end users. These were users who depended on natural gas for either feedstock or process needs. A fertilizer company is an example of the former and a textile finisher is an example of the latter. These users paid less than residential users, because their contract with a pipeline provided that they could be curtailed in certain circumstances. Curtailment in most cases, prior to 1974, would have meant plant shutdown. But curtailment had never occurred up to that time.

Lower down on the end user list were companies who could use an alternate fuel but preferred natural gas because of the price advantage over alternates. They were allowed an even lower rate for their gas but they were more liable to curtailment. Many did not have alternate fuel systems prior to 1974.

On the bottom of the list of interruptible users were those who used gas as a boiler fuel. These were mostly electric utilities, who were frequently curtailed during periods of peak heating demand in winter. All the electric utilities had alternate fuel capabilities.

The pipelines began to issue warnings of possible curtailment to industrial end users in 1974 and encouraged them to install alternate fuel systems where possible. Many of these companies went to considerable expense to do so. The majority of these companies were chagrined that these alternate systems saw little immediate use (even though they had cost a lot of money). The reason was that the winters of 1974 and 1975 were mild and there was almost no high priority curtailment.

Since there had been a fair amount of medium priority curtailment, some of these end users obtained FPC approval to purchase reserves in the ground. The FPC would allow these reserves to be transported by interstate pipeline for a period limited to two years. These purchases were permitted at the intrastate price, well above what the pipelines could pay.

The severe winters of 1976 through 1978 brought heavy curtailment to even highest priority industrial end users. Those who had complained about the cost of alternate fuel systems were glad that they had them and those who had not bought this "insurance" were shut down in many cases.

In 1976, the newly named Federal Energy Regulatory Commission permitted an increase in the price of regulated gas to $1.44 per MCF with a 1¢ per quarter escalator. Low priority usage of natural gas (primarily boiler fuel) was decried by the pipelines as a waste of a valuable depleting natural resource, although boiler fuel gas continued to be used to the extent of about 30% of total gas burned annually. Full price decontrol as an incentive to promote more gas exploration was a continuing campaign. Many industrial end users who did not have alternate fuel sources were encouraged once again to seek them. The watchwords to end users through 1978 were, "Conserve, seek alternates and clamor for decontrol."

Early in 1979, the gas supply situation had improved. This was due somewhat to the much-expanded exploration efforts which did show up in the wake of price increases. Much of the increased exploratory effort was expended by non-industrial end users; electric utilities, gas distribution companies and the interstate pipelines.

By early 1979, it appeared that two problems greater than natural gas curtailment were facing the United States: double digit inflation and distressing dependence on OPEC oil supplies. The Natural Gas Policy Act of 1978 had done away with the two-tier pricing system and had brought all natural gas pricing under the control of FERC. The American Gas Association continued to tell the public that their estimate was that there was three times more gas in the ground than had ever been burned.

By early 1979, new residential natural gas service was not only once again permitted, but encouraged in many areas. The price of natural gas was pegged around the $2.00 to $2.25 area, in spite of the fact that the parity with the mid-1979 OPEC oil price was approaching $4.00. It would appear that users were being given price encouragement to use gas instead of oil, when they had a choice. Whereas for the prior three years, the keynote had been "conserve," the word was now "use." Probably from a fiscal standpoint, (fighting inflation and the balance of payments problem) this was a wise choice.

In summary, the industrial end user had been warned of curtailments which did not come in 1974 to 1976. He was told to conserve and seek alternate fuels in the 1976 to 1978 period. Now the future, while not rosy in light of almost assuredly higher gas prices, looks less uncertain from the supply point of view. This was the 1974-1979 whipsaw of the industrial end user.

TWO VIABLE SOLUTIONS FOR YOUR FIRM

1. Direct purchase of reserves under Order #533

In August of 1975, the then-FPC issued Order #533, which made into policy what had been the Commission's practice for over a year. Order #533 permitted certain high priority end users to buy natural gas reserves from producers at the then higher intrastate prices. Control of who could benefit from such purchases was exercised by controlling the transportation of this gas. In order to transport gas across state lines, it is necessary to get what is called a "certificate of public necessity and convenience" to transport. Order #533 permitted the application for such transportation for a two year period.

Purchase under Order #533 was and is a stopgap measure. The end user-buyer under #533 was still at the mercy of increased prices after two years.

2. Direct end user involvement in gas exploration

In gas productive states, even prior to Order #533, a few gas end users had become involved directly in exploration programs. Their motivation was twofold: first, to have available an assured supply; second, to reduce their costs by taking a portion of the risk-taking explorationist's profits in the form of low cost gas instead of dollars. Transportation of the gas was no problem, since it involved only pipelines within the state.

Ohio, with its "self help" program has been the scene of many end user programs. The Ohio Department of Natural Resources has encouraged these programs. Other state utility commissions have encouraged exploration programs by permitting a surcharge (on all gas users) which is earmarked for exploration. In most cases, the exploration has been in conjunction with some stockholder investment by local gas distribution companies.

The largest intrastate end user program announced to date has been a joint venture between E.I. DuPont and Continental Oil. The purpose of DuPont in becoming a one-third partner in this $130 million three-year program in Texas was to find a lower cost dependable supply of gas to supply five fertilizer plants within the state.

In response to queries by numerous interstate end users about the possiblity of transporting reserves acquired by exploration, the FPC said that it would review such petitions on an individual basis. There was no assurance of being able to get more than a two year certificate to transport.

In spite of the question of transportation, one major company embarked on an exploration joint venture with two Texas operators. This was Burlington Industries, who committed $6 million to a three year program in 1976. Burlington's program was successful to the extent that it was reported in the Greensboro, NC, paper in March of 1978 that Burlington was taking some ten per cent of its natural gas needs as a direct result of exploration. This would entail a volume of about 2,500 MCF per day, since Burlington had been using about 25,000 MCF daily. Burlington obtained a two year certificate to transport in 1977 and obtained a renewal in 1979.

One other small exploration joint venture was formed in 1977 between a Texas operator and four end users in North Carolina and Virginia. This involved only $1,350,000 and no results have been announced as yet.

Probably the largest deterrent to end user exploration programs has been the lack of assurance—long-term assurance—of the ability to transport the reserves, once discovered.

There is, however, encouragement to be found, in the 1979 judicial finding in the "G.E. Case"—so-called by those who follow natural gas legislation and regulation. General Electric had purchased some existing reserves in place and had received permission to transport for a two year period. However, the fields producing the reserves warranted the drilling of some additional development wells. G.E. (and some of the pipelines which would be involved in transporting any gas found by those proposed development wells) petitioned the court for a judicial finding on the possibility of obtaining a 10 year certificate to transport this gas.

In 1979, the judge in the G.E. case recommended that a ten year certificate be granted on the basis that this would increase available natural gas and add to the energy supply of the nation. (The author's opinion is that the judge concurred that end user drilling was a constructive move and that it did not compete with the interstate pipelines whose creation was predicated upon purchase of gas from already producing wells.) Now this judicial opinion is, as stated, encouraging, but not binding. If the judicial finding is concurred with by the F.E.R.C. staff and commission members, then it is likely the ten year certificate will be granted. This would be an important precedent in natural gas transportation; a precedent that would hopefully encourage other end users to become active, based on the likelihood of obtaining 10 year permission to transport.

THE FUTURE OF END USER EXPLORATION PROGRAMS

The industrial end user who starts 1985 with an exploration-acquired reserve of natural gas will be far more competitive than the end user who will be paying the deregulated price (if there is no oil price hike) of $4 to $5 per MCF. The high priority user of natural gas for feedstock or process purposes will be able to benefit two ways from having locked up in the ground a reserve of this basic raw material in which it has a cost of 50¢ to $1 per MCF. Either it can price its end product lower than a competitor buying $5 market-priced gas (while still maintaining the same margin of profit) OR it can price its product the same as non-exploration advantaged competitors and increase its profit margin substantially, depending on how much of product cost is natural gas usage.

The only excuses for not participating in exploration for such a company are: 1) it cannot afford to invest the dollars or 2) it does not believe that natural gas prices will move substantially higher.

Budgeting dollars for the acquisition of natural gas by exploration is analogous to embarking on a self insurance program. The exploration program is a hedge against higher prices for natural gas, just as premiums are a hedge against claims which are sure to arise.

Problems of End User
Exploration Programs

The majority of problems associated with end user exploration programs are in dealing with the risks unknown to the company because it is not familiar with all facets of the oil business.

Here are most of those risks:

1. Legal (securities and taxes, possible partnership problem);
2. Accounting and auditing;
3. Negotiation with an operator;
4. Geological risks;
5. Acreage acquisition;
6. Fair pricing of drilling contracts;
7. Adequate communications from operator;
8. Reliable reserve reports upon development of properties;
9. Arrangement of transportation via pipeline.

Who Can Solve These Problems

1. Items 1 and 2 above can be taken care of by in-house counsel. The operating agreement can specify auditors acceptable to your firm's auditors.
2. Items 3 through 8 can be handled by a medium sized geological and engineering consulting firm. (They may need to use an outside landman for acreage evaluation or a corporate communications firm specializing in oil for items 5 and 7 respectively, but this can be made part of their consulting contract.)
3. Item 9, which is the most important item can be handled either with a transportation consultant or through your own attorneys. It is almost mandatory that either work through a Washington law firm experienced in obtaining certificates to transport gas.

CHECKLIST SHOWING HOW TO PLAN YOUR PROGRAM: MANAGING YOUR END USER PROGRAM

How to Plan Your Program

☐ 1. The owners or the board of directors must make a commitment to investing $1 million per year in a specified area of interest. (That area served by an interstate pipeline serving your area, if applicable.)

☐ 2. Such an authorization, in writing, will serve to evidence your seriousness in negotiating with other parties involved. The reason for having this written commitment is to convince those with whom you are negotiating that this is not a window shopping expedition. Enough of that has gone on in the past few years that ostensible interest on the part of an end user can be treated rather lightly by oil people.

☐ 3. If your bank is not an oil bank, ask for an introduction to one of their correspondents which has an oil department and is located in your area of interest. A relationship with the oil bank should be established by making a deposit of $25,000-$50,000 in some interest bearing type of account. Simultaneously set up a checking account with the purpose in mind of funneling all consultant's fees and exploration funding through this account. This will make your friendly new banker even more friendly. Use the oil department of your new bank to identify two or three independent consulting firms who can supply the expertise you need.

☐ 4. Inform your local gas distributor of your intended efforts and solicit their assistance. They will receive a transportation fee for hauling your gas and hopefully will be cooperative. At the same time, or possibly working through the distribution company, the interstate pipeline which serves you should also be informed. They likewise will receive a fee for hauling your gas, just as a truck line or railroad gets paid for hauling your finished product.

Since most interstate pipelines and many local gas distributors are involved in exploration, you may well be invited to participate with them on their joint ventures. Unless you are invited to participate on a "ground floor" basis, do not accept. By "ground floor", we mean without any promotion on the part of the pipeline or distributor. Otherwise, you will probably be burdened with a double promotion—that of the pipeline, who in turn will put your funds with another operator who will also receive a promotion. Double promotion is an acceptable means of achieving diversification when there is no alternative. With a budget of $1 million per year, you should be able to utilize at least half your money burdened only by a single promotion.

☐ 5. Assign responsibility to a single individual to see that communications snafus are avoided for the life of the program.

These five checkpoints are all *planning* decisions which involve:

1. The decision to pursue such a program;
2. The funding of the program;
3. The identifiication of expert consultants to assist in:
    a) making a choice of operator(s);
    b) negotiating terms of the program;
    c) advising on participation in individual prospects;
    d) advising on making completion expenditures;
    e) overseeing or providing communications;
    f) overseeing or providing reserve studies;
    g) overseeing or providing transportation arrangements.

How To Organize Your Program

1. Legal decisions

The form of your program should be a joint venture. Your operator or operators have somewhat different motivation from you. They want to produce a profit, regardless of where it comes from. You want to participate in prospects only in the area served by a pipeline coming to your facility. Therefore, you need the control of a joint venture—the right to participate in selected ventures which can produce gas for you if successful.

You must plan for the liabilities of a joint venture. Plan on being assessed for completion and development costs. Depending on your operator and the area of activity, you may be able to limit this under the terms of the joint venture to 50% or 100% of your original investment.

The legal liabilities can be somewhat covered by insurance. As a joint venturer, you can arrange in advance for the insurance carrier to advise you in advance if there is about to be a lapse in coverage. In the case of onshore drilling, most liabilities can be adequately covered by insurance.

If your company is closely-held and has a problem with the accumulation of surplus, the joint venture carries an additional benefit: as an *active* investment, the tax deductions which accrue will help to avoid further surplus accumulation.

2. Auditors

The choice of auditors can be a matter of mutual agreement between your firm and the operator's as part of the operating agreement.

3. Risk decisions

These will be made as part of your choice of operators. If you are seeking the lowest potential cost gas, rather than a higher priced, almost assured supply from proven properties, the choice of operators and their choice of area of activity will dictate the risk to which you are accepting exposure. Probably you should choose a widely diversified exploratory program. This way you know that seven or eight out of ten of the prospects drilled will be dry. However, the successful discoveries will yield additional development wells and should produce more reserves at a lessor cost over a period of time than you could hope for with drilling on proven properties.

Diversification in both number of prospects and time will be the greatest aids in mitigating the risk of exploratory drilling.

How to Activate and Control
Your End User Program

The planning and organization of your program will take care in advance of most of the details of the active phase of your program. Some important factors to be considered in such an arrangement, where the decision will be primarily controlled by your consultants, are:

1. A specified minimum number of prospects to be drilled per year. A minimum of 15 to 20 is suggested.
2. Right of first refusal on all prospects in predefined area of interest; final decision to rest with consultants; their bases for decision to be:
   (a) proximity to pipeline
   (b) geological merits and
   (c) economics.
3. Agreement in advance on communications. Daily drilling reports will not be informative in all likelihood. Brief quarterly reports in narrative form may be enough; you may want monthly reports. More often than once a month should be sufficient with interim reports of significant occurrences.
4. If there is any doubt in you or your auditors' mind about the total efficiency of the accounting ability of the operator's firm, perhaps you should give consideration to retaining an outside monitoring firm to double check on making bills dovetail exactly with AFE's.

SUGGESTIONS FOR CHOOSING AN OPERATOR

Although you are retaining consultants to assist in identifying an operator, if you can provide some guidelines for these consultants, it will make their job easier, less time-consuming and therefore less expensive for you. If you have some cash available, it is never any problem finding some operator to put it in the ground. Finding an operator who both meets your criteria *and* who wants to accept the limitations you wish to impose on him is not so easy.

Your search for an operator for your end user program should be limited to those who can provide:

1. Ten years' experience in the area of activity;
2. A "substantial" balance sheet— this is your judgment;
3. A well documented record of gas-finding costs;
4. A drilling budget in which your investment will be no less than 3-5% nor more than 10-15% of total. This means that for an anticipated $1 million per year investment the operator should be planning a budget of $10-$25 million;
5. Some portion of the risk money—drilling costs to the casing point;
6. A large enough technical staff to originate at least half the prospects drilled during your time of involvement.

It almost goes without saying that when the choice is narrowed down to two or three, that it is important for you and your staff to get to know both the principals and staff of the operators under consideration. Since you are entering into a proposed three year program, it is important, insofar as possible, to design out potential conflicts of personality.

It is evident by now that the above criteria will narrow the field of prospective operators considerably. Even though there are some 10,000 oil companies, these guidelines will cull out all but about a hundred. There have been about 150 industrial companies who have been involved in using natural gas purchased under the two year Order #533 contract. They are all potential investors in end user programs. If they all decide to set up their own end user programs, then the market will reverse for end users.

As it stands now, most operators of the size under consideration would be most cooperative in conforming to the strictures imposed by a three year commitment of $1 million per year. You, the end user, are currently in a buyers' market. It can become a sellers' market (from the standpoint of operators) in a very short time if only half the end users buying #533 gas decide to become direct participants in exploration. How could this affect a procrastinating end user?

Here are some of the blue sky limitations that an operator, if it met the criteria in the proceeding discussion, might impose on potential end user—investors in the middle 1980s.

1. No less than two million per year committed for five years.
2. Participation in all prospects, regardless of propinquity to pipelines, with penalties (e.g., 300% for non-consent).
3. Advance payments at first of year to cover overhead billings to follow.
4. End users may participate only as limited partners, giving up all right to manage or control the program.

By the time this kind of hypothesis is confirmed—say, 1985—you may be paying $6 to $8 per MCF, while your foresighted competitor is using gas he got by exploration in 1981 that cost him less than $1.

HOW MUCH MONEY SHOULD AN END USER COMMIT?

A rough guideline is to plan to invest about $4 million for every million cubic feet per day you hope to have deliverable. That is, $1 million per year for three years, plus about $1 million in completion costs. There may be some further cash drain brought on by the necessity of paying royalties to landowners on gas which you take in kind. This will probably be covered by the wells which produce oil which will be sold. These are ball park figures for a program onshore in the Texas and Louisiana gulf coast. Your consultant can further refine these for the area of anticipated interest and the operator you will be working with.

THE BOTTOM LINE: HOW AN END USER PROFITS FROM LOW COST GAS

This is not an attempt at an accounting lesson, but outlines how low cost gas acquired by exploration may be treated.

Take the gas into inventory at finding cost, probably on a last-in-first-out basis. Book the inventory cost into the selling price of your product and report the increased profit for tax purposes. A second alternative would be to price your product more competitively (which you can do, due to your lower costs) and make a higher profit on greater volume, if your product line works this way.

The First Step

Mail a copy of this chapter to your board or stockholders prior to your next meeting.

9

Advice From The Pros

To give you a good idea as to what goes on in the minds of the pros we will show you in this chapter how some of the leading investors in the field operate.

The author extends appreciation to:

Fred E. Newberg, Senior Vice President and Director, Butcher and Singer Inc. (parent company of Energysearch) for his comments on their investment goals and strategies;

John Brasher, Executive Vice President of Can Am Securities, for permission to reprint his comments on the importance of track record;

Investment Dealer's Digest® for their permission to reprint an article on the importance of professional monitoring written by the late David A. Gracer and Steven H. Saperstein of the David Gracer Company.

It is not the author's intent to endorse any program herein but only just to share any philosophies and strategies of experienced program operators and investment counsellors.

FRED E. NEWBERG

Investment Goals and
Strategies

The following comments by a Senior Vice President and Director, Butcher and Singer, Inc. (parent company of Energysearch) will show some of the investment goals and strategies behind development and exploration programs.

I. General Description and Background

The Energysearch Division of Butcher & Singer Inc. is a successful and active oil and gas exploration and development group which drills and operates in most of the onshore producing regions of the United States and Canada. Since 1972 we have drilled more than 700 wells. Exploration activities have been concentrated in the Rocky Mountain and Gulf Coast areas of the United States and in Alberta, Canada. Development activities have been principally conducted in the Appalachian Basin area of the United States.

Funding for this drilling has come primarily from the sale of limited partnership interests by a group of investment banking firms throughout the U.S., including Butcher & Singer Inc., the parent of Energysearch. Since 1972 we have formed some 70 partnerships to carry out our drilling projects. Energysearch, which has grown steadily over the past seven years, now ranks as one of the largest fund-raisers for oil and gas drilling in the investment banking industry.

In 1979, Energysearch has a drilling budget of about $50 million. Approximately half of this dollar volume will be raised through partnerships registered with the United States Securities and Exchange Commission. The balance will come through private placements to both individuals and institutions.

II. Exploration Activities

In the exploration drilling conducted since 1972, our partnerships have made significant oil or gas finds in Alberta, Canada and in New Mexico, Colorado, Nebraska, Texas and Utah in the United States. As an example, a well drilled in Leon County, Texas in 1977 by one of our partnerships was recently sold (including two development wells and about 7,000 acres under lease) for about $5 million. It should be pointed out that this was for the partnership's 25 percent interest in this particular prospect. An overriding royalty interest was retained by our partnership.

Part of our exploration strategy is that each partnership should participate in a large enough number of wells to permit a reasonable number of chances and to, in our opinion, enhance the risk/reward ratio. While our exploration partnerships consist entirely of exploratory wells, we do try to choose a balance of depth and risk within the exploratory spectrum. Of the ten exploration partnerships we have formed in the last seven years, our best return on investment (based on independent engineering) from a partnership is about 16 to one—per $1,000,000 investment, and expected future net revenue of $16 million. Average exploratory return is currently averaging around five to one for all ten of these partnerships, including two partnerships in which it appears there will not be a positive return. All of these figures are based on current prices with an assumed inflation rate of about 7 percent.

III. Development Activities

Our developmental drilling operations began modestly in 1975. The interest in this type of drilling, however, has been so strong that it has grown not only in absolute but also percentage volume and now comprises more than 80 percent of our total drilling budget. When the decision was reached to seek out developmental drilling opportunities, we reviewed and considered a number of developmental or semi-developmental areas. Our choice ultimately was the Appalachian Basin—primarily in the states of Ohio, West Virginia and Pennsylvania. This choice was made for several reasons:

1. low risk
2. high predictability of recoverable reserves;
3. low drilling cost, permitting the drilling of large numbers of wells so that averages could be achieved, and
4. availability of large acreage blocks at relatively low cost.

With this said, the obvious question must be, if profitable production is so easily available in the Appalachian area, then why doesn't everyone else drill there? The answer, naturally, is not so simple as the question. First, profitable production is not all that easily available. Only through careful choosing of prospects and extremely careful negotiation with drillers and land owners, along with stringent cost controls, can this area be profitable. Clearly, everyone does not want to bother with all these problems.

Another part of the answer to the question, "Why Appalachian drilling?" must look to the geological characteristics of the area. In evaluating a proposed drilling venture in the Appalachian Basin, the considerations vary somewhat from those in a more exploratory area. First, the geological configuration of the area is depositional in nature and the oil and gas bearing sand deposits extend in blanket type layers over broad areas, differing mainly in thickness and porosity. This blanket sand characteristic means that in a given area, if the thickness and porosity have been determined from drilling several wells, the average of those wells is likely to indicate what the average sand thickness and porosity will be on the other wells drilled in that particular area.

Also, actual production data from nearby wells, which is available in this area, provides the best indicator of the type of production likely to be encountered by other wells drilled in close proximity. (Again because of the blanket type subsurface structure.) It should be noted that because of the low porosity and permeability of producing formations in this area, little migration of oil or gas occurs, and therefore, nearby wells are a positive indicator of productive capacity and not likely to have depleted nearby locations. In fact, only in areas such as this that are not depleted, but still have location available that *directly offset* other producing wells, do we believe the drilling is truly developmental.

Now the question expands to, "What does all this mean to the overall economics of Appalachian Drilling and why can Energysearch approach this drilling on a profitable and successful basis?"

The total reserves of any group of wells in, for example, Ohio (allowing for individual variation) are greatly predictable. This means that given whatever pricing assumptions one thinks reasonable, the total gross return on any given group of wells in this area can be far more accurately predicted than almost anywhere in the United States. Assuming we have chosen drilling in an attractive area with adequate production data from nearby wells, we can make fairly accurate reserve estimates in advance. Therefore, the terms of the transaction become one of the most important factors to the investor, and also, the reason why everyone is not doing this type of drilling as successfully as Energysearch.

In order to obtain favorable terms, the investor, or general partner-organizer of a drilling program must be dealing in sufficiently large volume to be able to exert some leverage over the drillers, and for the drillers to be able to operate profitably at close margins, they must have confidence that these volume levels will be met. Therefore, only a group such as Energysearch which, first, understands these facts; and second, has a major commitment to Appalachian drilling, is able to trade the most favorable arrangements for its investors.

Specifically, terms of a drilling program must be analyzed at two levels—price and carried interests. The price of drilling varies widely but Energysearch has taken the approach that rather than rely on fixed-price contracts which might include unknown profits to operators, we would prefer to pay costs of drilling on an invoice basis with a prenegotiated profit to the drillers which tends to run in the range of 6 percent to 10 percent. This compares to other operators charging fixed or "turnkey" prices of 25 percent to 100 percent over costs. We believe this feature gives us the built-in advantage of getting more wells drilled per dollar spent.

On the carried interest side, it is important to look not only at carried working interest but also any overriding royalty burdens paid to third parties, because the ultimate return to an investor is net of all such outstanding interests. What level of promotion or carried interest a drilling venture will stand depends on the expectation of reserves, but an easy rule of thumb for Appalachian drilling is that the NET REVENUE INTEREST TO INVESTORS should not dip below 70 percent to 75 percent of all revenues from production. All of our development partnerships have stayed within these bounds.

As a measure of the success of this approach to development drilling in the Appalachian region, independent engineering of reserves discovered in all of the 18 development drilling partnerships organized by this firm in 1975 and 1976 (our first two years of development drilling) indicate an average return on investment of 2.8 to 1 over the expected life of these partnerships. Averages obviously are not only meaningful if the particular investment one chooses meets or exceeds that average. In our case, however, we believe that the average of these early partnerships is particularly meaningful to today's investor. This is because our first two years of operation represented to some extent a winnowing process which permitted us to determine the most attractive areas for this type of development drilling.

A final advantage to the development drilling we engage in which derives from our planning and experience is the early cash flow available as compared with either exploratory drilling or less carefully managed development drilling. Our average time span between investment and cash flow from sale of production is about one year. Average return of the first invested dollar can be expected in four to five years from date of investment. This factor has a very positive effect on the internal rate of return because the investor has the use of his invested funds back early plus a continuing income stream.

This early cash flow is accomplished by drilling in areas where pipeline availability (for natural gas) is good; maintaining good relationships with the gas utilities; maintaining close supervision of operations; and finally, by our willingness to do whatever is necessary to bring wells on to production including building our own pipelines when other alternatives are not available. In fact we have done this on several occasions when the quality of the drilling prospects was sufficient to persuade us to drill in areas not already directly served by pipelines.

Success in Appalachian development drilling comes from a variety of factors which include selection of leases and operators; scrutiny of the available production data from nearby wells; very careful cost controls; the trading of more favorable terms than are ordinarily available, based on the ability to deal in large volume; and lastly and importantly, an intangible factor of experience, which ultimately makes it possible to achieve all these other things.

IV. Administration and Communications

The ability to provide sufficient and consistent administration and communication is a rather unglamorous but extremely important factor in the continued success of any enterprise. When managing a large number of partnerships in very disparate geographical areas, with different groups of investors, good administration takes on an even greater importance. At Energysearch, a staff of business professionals, accountants and attorneys, backed up by advanced computer technology and a staff to utilize this computer ability to its utmost, provide the administrative skills and commitment necessary for the high quality continuing management of partnerships and the communication with investors on which we place such importance.

As to communications, we believe it is imperative to provide reports to investors, even in more mature partnerships at least every three months. During the drilling phase of partnerships, we report with even greater frequency. These reports must be in clear, understandable language to investors who may not be conversant in oil and gas terminology. Also, these reports provide a summary of activities to date in addition to current information, thus providing investors with a complete picture of their partnership's activities.

V. Investment Goals

The programs developed by our oil and gas division are targeted for the special client, the individual whose tax bracket and net worth necessitate sound investment and sophisticated tax planning. Our goal is to offer to our sales force, our clients and to the industry programs that accomplish the following:

1. Preserve existing capital and build future net worth;
2. Provide a better than average return on investment in comparison with other investment opportunities;
3. Fight inflation; and
4. Provide maximum tax benefits without sacrificing the economics of the investment

DAVID A. GRACER AND STEVEN H. SAPERSTEIN

Professional Monitoring

The following article from Investment Dealers' Digest will show the importance behind professional monitoring of oil and gas investments, how it works, and the steps that go into monitoring.

Many investors view an oil and gas drilling program in the same way as they regard their investments in stocks and bonds. Oil and gas investments, however, are different. Programs invariably involve many wells; each generally costs form $250,000 to $2,000,000. A single exploration effort is akin to starting a new business, with expenses involved in hundreds of individual transactions. These usually span several months during the drilling period, whether or not the effort is successful. If successful, it can be expected to require accounting for revenues and expenses over a span of many years, and many even involve drilling several more wells, each with its own multitude of transactions. Accounting for revenues from wells is not a simple matter either. It is to be expected, and our experience has shown, that a certain percentage of reporting and accounting errors will occur in such a vast number of transactions.

Those who participate in oil and gas drilling programs are seldom in a position to make a detailed review of the activities of the oil companies which act as general partners (operators) of the programs. For one thing, an investor doesn't usually have the time or the knowledge to evaluate the many records and reports on drilling activity. Indeed, he isn't likely to recognize an abnormal situation, nor feel strongly enough about his point of view to challenge the operator (assuming he knows what to challenge). Even accountants auditing a program's financial statements are not expected to review certain operations and reports necessary to fully protect the investors' interest. To illustrate, auditors would not review whether a partnership should have participated with the operator in purchasing additional acreage near a partnership discovery.

Monitoring is a necessary procedure—it has a lot in common with the review made by an oil company of another oil company's operations for their joint account. While the monitoring personnel should deal cordially and professionally with the operators, they should not be beholden to them. Their only concern should be to protect and enhance the investments of their clients who have committed funds to drilling programs.

Periodic trips should be made to operators' main and divisional offices, and occasionally to the well sites. These give the monitoring staff an opportunity to establish rapport with the operator and its personnel at many different levels. The operators come to realize through these contacts that their investors are seriously interested in maximum return on their investment, and that operations and reports will be examined carefully, rather than accepted blindly. Thus, monitoring is preventive medicine, since the operators know their policies and practices will be reviewed by an authoritative outside party. Frequent contact between the monitoring staff and the operators leads to more prompt and meaningful disclosure of problems.

Management and personnel of the operators are characteristically honest. Nevertheless, they sometimes make errors in carrying out their agreements, often running in favor of the operator and against the investors' interest, and sometimes issue incomplete and inaccurate reports. Monitoring has often spurred operators to make corrections materially benefiting their investors. However innocent or inadvertent errors may be, they can divert substantial sums of money which would otherwise flow to the investors.

While operators have a fiduciary responsibility to their investors, their staffs cannot always be expected to perform checking operations. First of all, they do not have the incentive to do so. Additionally, the operator's staff is unlikely to be more loyal to the investors than to its own employer. While not necessarily intended, employees can be expected from time to time to succumb to the natural tendency to give their employer the benefit of the doubt when making decisions which involve a conflict of interest, and in reporting to investors.

There is no guarantee monitoring will always be able to ascertain improprieties or inaccuracies. The occasions on which inaccuracies or inconsistencies are found normally are far outnumbered by those where none are discovered. Most operators' reports may be accepted as submitted, after being checked.

Examples of Problems Dealt With By Monitoring

Errors frequently may be discovered deriving from the application of incorrect cost and revenue sharing ratios. Because of the complexity of accounting for drilling operations where more than one party participates in the costs of drilling, and where more than one will participate in revenues if and when wells become productive, there are numerous possibilities for error. The likelihood is increased when an unusual degree of complexity is introduced into the financial arrangements, such as when costs are divided on a "functional allocation" basis, allocating a higher share of items which are tax deductible to limited partners; and when there are several interests in a lease or prospect, each may be subject to different agreements.

Other errors may derive from the fact that the operator is often involved in drilling and operating a number of other wells for its own account, and for the accounts of others. Charges on non-program wells made to a program, incorrect statements of capital contributions, and erroneous reports have also been frequently observed by us.

And, as previously implied, investors have sometimes not been included in purchase of acreage based on their partnerships' discoveries.

How Does Monitoring Work?

The heart of monitoring is the review of joint interest billings (JIBs). These are statements which list all prospect, lease and well expenses, from pumping units to cotter pins. Revenues from production must be scrutinized as closely as expenses; this is normally accomplished with the assistance of charts and graphs. Daily drilling reports, authorities for expenditure, plats, revenue and working interest calculations, gas contracts, and financial statements are other important sources of information.

Monitoring involves constant comparison: between an operator's reports to investors and State records; between daily drilling reports and JIBs; between financial statements and tax returns; between revenue statements and gas contracts. Concern for detail and constant follow-up are a must. Some matters require review only once; others from time to time, on a random basis; still others, continuously. The business aspects of each program dictate the frequency and depth of review advisable for various kinds of transactions.

Lawyers, accountants and petroleum geologists or engineers should be available to the monitoring staff to help interpret agreements, resolve tax questions, advise on assessments, amendments or other similar matters. Monitors should not rely solely on information provided by the operators, but try to obtain independent verification by corresponding with State regulatory agencies and with contractors who provide materials and services for the wells. Acquaintances with the personnel of many oil and gas companies, and review of industry publications, are also good sources of information on developments in the geological areas of interest of a program's wells.

ABBREVIATED LIST OF MONITORING ACTIVITIES

1. Review books, records and correspondence.
2. Review reports, letters, memoranda and projections submitted to investors by operators.
3. Visit operators' offices and fields.
4. Review operators' files for opinions of counsel on drillsites, inclusion of proper State authorizations and other pertinent information.
5. Review daily drilling reports.
6. Review proposals to acquire acreage and operators' non-program activity in and around areas of interest.

7. Review working and revenue interest calculations.
8. Review need for remedial work undertaken on wells.
9. Review proposals to waterflood.
10. Confer with banks.
11. Review loan payments and calculations of interest.
12. Review oil and gas sales prices.
13. Review gas sales contracts, and diary price redetermina ion dates.
14. Review oil and gas production.
15. Review variance between budgeted and actual costs.
16. Review leasehold costs.
17. Review for proper allocation of expenses to accounts of investors.
18. Review pipe purchases and warehouse stocks.
19. Review relevant books and records for credit to investors of their share of salvage, and contributions by others toward drilling.
20. Review lease operating expenses.
21. Review overhead charges.
22. Review legal and accounting costs.
23. Correspond with State authorities to verify issuance of permits to drill, plug, etc.
24. Correspond with vendors to verify they provided services and materials.
25. Correspond with oil and gas purchasers to verify takes and prices.
26. Review insurance coverage.
27. Review investment of temporary cash surpluses.
28. Review reserve estimates and changes in reserves.
29. Review audited and unaudited financial reports and partnership tax returns.
30. Review operators' press releases, stockholders reports and SEC filings.

Monitoring Activities Auditors Are Not Expected To Perform

1. Determine that adequate insurance was obtained to protect the partnership.
2. Determine that opinion of counsel on title to leases was obtained prior to drilling.
3. Review drilling operations on a day-to-day basis.
4. Review JIBs, and compare costs with DDRs, AFEs, etc.
5. Independently check that wells are drilled, tested and plugged (through Railroad Commission, county clerks, vendors, etc.)
6. Determine that acreage, dry hole and bottom hold contributions by others are proportionately credited to investors.
7. Review waterflood, rework, etc.
8. Determine that division orders are timely signed.
9. Review assessments, and recommend whether to participate.
10. Review acreage position for development drilling potential.
11. Determine that the operator included the partnership in geologically related acreage purchased after a partnership is formed.
12. Review oil and gas production, and investigate reasons for abnormal decreases.
13. Review dropped acreage, and who acquired it.
14. Diary gas price redetermination dates.
15. Verify changes in working and revenue interest percentages, based on operation agreements.
16. Periodically review estimates of investors, or placed in interest-bearing accounts for future partnership use.
18. Review buy-out offers, and recommend whether acceptance is advisable.
19. Review and recommend amendments to agreements.

JOHN BRASHER

The following comments by the President of Can Am Securities will illustrate the importance of track record from the standpoint of building reserves in the ground.

Exploration—The Key To High Potential

Finding and developing large significant commercial reserves of oil and natural gas can only be accomplished by a well managed, properly diversified, exploration program operating in areas that have the proper statistical risk-reward ratios. Companies do not grow dramatically nor do partnerships tend to have multiple returns when operations are conducted near the edges of previously discovered reserves.

Track records (or performance) are not built by drilling wells but by discovering new reserves of oil and gas. One hundred wells drilled in a 50 year old field could be successful but the partner might not make a profit due to the field being significantly depleted as to the reserves (amounts of oil and gas left to produce). Exploration involves the acquisition of hopefully a sizable acreage position located over an area of a suspected hydrocarbon trap. The exploration well is then drilled. If successful, then all of the acreage in the area belongs to the partner who risked his money to drill the discovery well. Exploration companies are in business to discover fields not wells. The ultimate development (or additional drilling) will then maximize your ultimate return.

Investors desiring to build wealth through the conversion of highly taxable ordinary income into capital assets (oil and gas in the ground) should participate over a period of time with a well managed and *equitable* exploration program. History has proved time and time again that companies and partnerships have been significantly successful due to a few (perhaps one) large discoveries annually or even over their history. But the key is continued participation in a well diversified program (assuming management is capable).

There are three keys to building wealth in the oil and gas industry—capable people, an adequate budget, and a period of time. No one company has success on all of their ventures, but provided the above criteria are met, that company will make money looking for oil and natural gas.

However, the wealth should grow much more rapidly if the company's primary emphasis is on exploration and development of it's own successes.

There are many definitions in the oil industry. Exploration, basically, is the search for hydrocarbons where they have not previously been located. This could be deeper in a field that is already producing from shallow zones or vice-versa. It could be in new frontier areas where hydrocarbons have yet to be discovered, or it could be an extension of previously known areas. Oil and gas are located beneath the earth's surface but are normally discovered by new ideas generated by geologists and geophysicists. Remember, all the science in the world to date has not been able to ascertain whether a well will be productive before it is drilled (even a development well).

In a properly managed exploration program, diversification in areas that are statistically sound is of utmost importance. Each well drilled by a company is drilled on a risk—reward (or a dollar in-dollar out) ratio. Management poses this question—"Geologically, if we're right; how many dollars will I get back for every dollar spent?" If the ratio is 50 to 1, 75 to 1, 100 to 1; it's not hard to see that if successful a few dry holes can be drilled subsequently and the company will still make money.

Drilling in more remote areas and deeper drilling statistically has outshined traditional shallow to medium exploration in the past decade. The reason being, of course, is that the more traditional areas have been picked over and the chance to find substantial reserves diminishes with this fact. Large capital commitments are required for these deeper and more remote projects, and a publicly registered program, which has been scrutinized closely before being offered to the public, is one of the few ways to participate in the high potential areas. Individual wells in some of these areas cost up to $8 million to drill, but reserves per well could equal $150 million (50 BCF @ $3.00/mcf) or more.

It's not hard to visualize as a limited partner that if you owned 1/1,000,000 of everything a major oil company had done through its history you would have been well rewarded. So it is with an exploration program. Participation on an averaging basis over a period of time could bring adequate rewards and a track record that would be hard to beat. We in the oil and gas industry are in business to reap substantial rewards, not to shelter highly taxed incomes. With current prices ($42.00/bbl) for oil and ($2.50/mcf to $6.00/mcf) for natural gas, the chance for high potential and lesser risk (due to the net economics) are better than ever in our history. Beyond all my doubt, a properly managed exploration program will average, as we say, "Many Happy Returns."

Appendix

Now that you have learned all about drilling programs, here is a list of some of the brokerage firms who handle them. These firms have years of experience in evaluating oil programs, have a reputation for not only thorough due diligence studies, but also for an on-going interest in these programs on behalf of their clients.

National Firms—address of headquarters

E.F. Hutton & Co., Inc.
1 Battery Park Plaza
New York, NY 10004

The acknowledged leader in the field of tax shelter investments, they have sold over $1 billion in this highly competitive market.

Merrill Lynch Pierce Fenner & Smith Incorporated
One Liberty Plaza
New York, NY 10006

Paine Webber Jackson & Curtis, Incorporated
140 Broadway
New York, NY 10005

Bache Halsey Stuart Shields Incorporated
100 Gold St.
New York, NY 10038

Dean Witter Reynolds Inc.
45 Montgomery St.
San Francisco, CA 94106

Smith Barney Harris Upham & Co., Incorporated
1345 Ave. of the Americas
New York, NY 10019

Thomson McKinnon Securities Inc.
One New York Plaza
New York, NY 10004

A.G. Edwards & Sons Inc.
One N. Jefferson Ave., PO Box 14754
St. Louis, MO 63178

Regional Firms—address of headquarters

Rotan Mosle Inc.
Pennzoil Plaza, 1000 S. Tower
Houston, TX 77002

Although small compared to the national firms, Rotan Mosle does significant oil financing, including originating and marketing drilling programs.

Rauscher Pierce Refnes Inc.
1200 Mercantile Dallas Bldg.
Dallas, TX 75201

Piper Jaffrey & Hopwood Incorporated
800 Multifoods Bldg.
Minneapolis, MN 55402

Butcher & Singer Inc.
1500 Walnut St.
Philadelphia, PA 19102

Drexel Burnham Lambert Incorporated
60 Broad St.
New York, NY 10004

INDEX